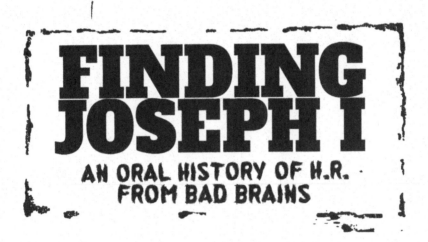

FINDING JOSEPH I

AN ORAL HISTORY OF H.R. FROM BAD BRAINS

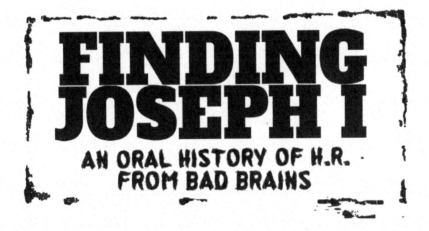

FINDING JOSEPH I

AN ORAL HISTORY OF H.R. FROM BAD BRAINS

HOWIE ABRAMS
JAMES LATHOS

Post Hill
PRESS

A POST HILL PRESS BOOK
ISBN: 978-1-64293-195-2
ISBN (eBook): 978-1-64293-196-9

Finding Joseph I:
An Oral History of H.R. from Bad Brains
© 2019 by Howie Abrams and James Lathos
All Rights Reserved

Published by arrangement with Overamstel Publishers, Inc.

Post Hill Press
New York • Nashville
posthillpress.com

Published in the United States of America

TABLE OF CONTENTS

FOREWORD

In 1989, I was an eighteen-year-old punk rock-obsessed kid living in the Tidewater area of Virginia. My long-suffering girlfriend would often accompany me to shows in Virginia Beach and Norfolk. Much to her dismay, once the music started, I would inevitably take off my spike-covered punk rock jacket and wallet, hand them to her, and say "Will you hold this for a second, honey? I gotta go dance, just for one song—I promise I'll be right back, okay?" Then I would promptly disappear into the slam pit for the rest of the night, leaving her holding my stuff. What a jerk.

In the days leading up to one particular show we were both very excited about, my girlfriend made me promise several times that when we went out that night, I wouldn't pull my usual vanishing act. She was sick of my testosterone-on-overdrive antics. She was a music fan, too, and she wanted to watch the bands without having to hold all my crap in a steaming hot club while I ran around smashing into a bunch of other sweaty dudes.

"I'm not a coat rack, Randy," she said. Fair enough.

On August 15, 1989, we drove to a club in Virginia Beach called The Jetty. The show was packed, and the opening acts, Leeway and Corrosion of Conformity both put on stellar high-energy sets, but I stood dutifully beside my lady towards the back of the club, good to my word. Then the headliner took the stage, the amps started to hum, and without warning, the band burst into my favorite song. That song was "Re-ignition," and the band was Bad Brains. Before she had a chance to even utter the word "No!," my jacket was in her arms and I was gone. (I'm sorry, lady.)

It was, and remains to this day, the best show I have ever seen in my life.

The musicians played with a conviction you felt on a visceral level—their music shook the audience into an ecstatic state. And the front man, H.R., had a stage presence that was literally life-altering to witness. The man moved and sang like a human lightning rod, as if he were communicating with the heavens, channeling some sort of vast cosmic power through his voice and body. You had to be there in person to understand it, to feel it in the air on a molecular level—to see H.R. fronting Bad Brains while he was still at the peak of his powers was like watching a man reaching up and tearing the sky in two with his bare hands. It was unbelievable. I've seen a few thousand shows since that night, but I've never seen any other front man come even remotely close to that level of intensity. Not one.

Countless other folks, including the people in this book, will tell you the exact same story. H.R. is a living legend for a reason.

But legends, living or not, always carry the weight of story. And over the years, I began to hear many, many stories about H.R., most of them involving rather bizarre behavior, both on- and offstage. At first, these weird tales were amusing, as I assumed them merely the antics of a highly gifted but eccentric artist. (I've known several of these types over the years and, admittedly, there is certainly something a little "off" about most of us creative sorts.) A lot of those stories I wrote off as hearsay, just the inevitable gossip that always develops around any person with a fanbase. But eventually, I began hearing things from people who had been close to H.R. and Bad Brains throughout the years, and the stories were no longer funny to me. Someone needs to help that man, I would think, because something has obviously gone severely wrong in his psyche. As an alcoholic who drank himself to the very edge of madness before sobering up several years ago, I have empathy for people who suffer when their mind turns against them. I've been there and it's a terrifying place. I got some help, and I'm so glad I did, as I am certain I would be dead now if I hadn't. But with every new crazy story I would hear about H.R., I would think grim thoughts. Man, I hope that dude makes it. He doesn't sound long for this earth.

Incredibly, H.R. made it. This book tells that story. It is a tale of surviving a deadly head-on battle with the ultimate foe—the darkest part of oneself that lives within us all. It's a miracle the man is alive today.

After H.R.'s recent brain surgery to treat his headaches, I had the indescribable honor of performing some of the faster songs in the set at a few Bad Brains shows. Singing with my favorite band of all time was amazing, albeit highly daunting. How are you supposed to fill the shoes of the greatest front man of all time? You aren't—it's impossible. But I did my best to honor the music that means so much to me, viewing my poor efforts as returning some of the life-affirming energy the band gave me in the first place, of helping to keep the circle of P.M.A. flowing while the originator healed up. In the process, I have gotten to know H.R. a bit. He is a magnificent and deeply complex human being. There is something very special about this man, and I am so happy to report that from my firsthand experience, he is in a much better mental state now.

In preparation for writing this introduction, I reread this book and re-watched the excellent documentary by the same name that this project grew from. It was hard for me to read some of the stories and to watch some of the footage of H.R. caught in some of his darkest moments—that person is not the warm, centered, exceedingly gentle man that I have come to know. But I also know that those moments were real; a painful segment of his continuing story. I applaud him for having the guts to share those dark times so openly and publicly, for I believe that by sharing our stories, both happy and sad, we can bring hope for a better day to others who suffer.

Isn't that what the Bad Brains were trying to tell us all along? To maintain hope in the face of despair? "Don't care what they may do, we got that attitude … " Thank you for singing those words, H.R. This kid listened, took them to heart, and they helped him more than you can know.

And, yes, I do have that P.M.A.

One love—

D. Randall Blythe

"Greetings in the name of His Imperial Majesty, Selassie I the first, Jah Rastafari, Almighty One, King of Kings, Lord of Lords, Conquering Lion of the Tribe of Judah, Elect of Himself, Earth's Rightful Ruler, Holy, Jesus Christ the Messiah."

-H.R.

"**Back in the day, H.R. used to have a staff and walk around with a rod. So H.R. meant 'Hunting Rod' before it developed into 'Human Rights.'"**

-EARL HUDSON
BAD BRAINS, HUMAN RIGHTS, H.R.'S BROTHER

"In the 12 Tribes of Israel, every man is born a month, and each month has its own tribe. The significance of 'Joseph' in the Bible… That love for everybody. Him get the name Joseph from that."

-RAS MICHAEL
SONS OF NEGUS

PROLOGUE

The following excerpts are taken from interviews conducted by filmmaker James Lathos with H.R. in Jamaica between February 4 and 14, 2012.

JAMES LATHOS: Tell us who you are.

H.R.: Okay. I'm Mr. PhD, more commonly known as Mr. Paul D. Hudson. My friends call me H.R., short for "Hunting Rod" or "Human Rights," and formerly I was called "Ras Hailu Gabriel Joseph I." I want to thank you again for believing in I and I, and for just everything. It's been most approvable. We find your peace offering approvable, and your love, and also your words of inspiration most acceptable. Thank you again. Jah[1] Love, Rastafari.

JAMES: I want you to explain some things to me, because I care about you. I filmed you that one week in Baltimore and you painted your face . . .

H.R.: (Laughs knowingly.)

JAMES: . . . and you wore a robe out in public. I don't know where you are sometimes and can't connect with you. A lot of people say you're just being an artist. Other people think you're sick. Can you explain what happens to you when these things that people talk about happen?

---

[1] *Jah: the Rastafarian name of God*

H.R.: I think it was, more or less, trying to be as awesome and unpredictable as possible. At times—I did not really know how I would be received and what the response would be, and the only way I could find out was by doing it—and so that's what I did. It had some very interesting responses to it. It was a bit unpredictable and a bit unadulterated, and some people didn't even recognize me. They had no idea who it was, and I could hear their opinion on what was going on. And so, for me, it was interesting to hear. I don't know if people were telling the truth or not, but they said some pretty wild things. And once I knew what they were saying, I just took my wig off and put it aside, and didn't use as much makeup, and eventually, it got kind of put away and I don't know where it went. That was that.

JAMES: So, you're just trying to fuck with people? Going out like that to see how people might react. Is that what it is?

H.R.: No, no. I knew I had to lighten up. I was given an objective.

JAMES: So, are you trying to shock people by dressing like that?

H.R.: No. I wanted to be more of that kind of person that I felt inside, or what I knew inside, and was given to me to lighten up the idea. One of the former managers said, "Spruce yourself up and lighten up, dude. Don't slap people in the face, because your dreads are so gnarly." I said, "Okay, let me see what I can do," and I went over to the place where they had hairpieces and got me this blonde hairpiece, and got me some makeup. I had gotten the idea from Dennis Rodman. I learned later through experience in life that you can't fool all the people all the time, and you can't make everybody happy, but if you try, sometimes you get what you need. Don't look back; keep moving forward, and that's what I did. I kept on moving forward. Thank goodness, because to my surprise, people loved me. They didn't love the hairpiece, and they didn't love the makeup. They loved me and they loved the music, and now they wanted to know who I was. Where was the band coming from? Who were the Brains? Who were the mighty Brains? Who was Human Rights? Who is that individual inside that individual? Am I pretending to be H.R., or am I really, truly, you know, Dr. PhD? And so that is basically where it's coming from.

JAMES: Well, who are you? Paul Hudson, Joseph I, Dr. PhD, H.R.?

H.R.: I am what I am. I do love to be happy—and at one with God and the audience, and I don't want to be a threat to anybody's existence, so for that reason, we became more in tune with a universal love and a proper understanding.

JAMES: Tell me about your brother. He has to be your best friend.

H.R.: I wanted him to be my drummer and I wanted to be his vocalist, and nobody else would play those songs with me except for Earl. I remember telling Earl he was massive, he was just incredible, but he worries about everything. I mean, he sees A through Z. He's always been an inspiration and always a very direct individual. Conscious, clean, upright. He does have different ideas. Some of his ideals are more majestic rounded.

JAMES: Do you pretend a lot?

H.R.: Oh, that's my second name: Mr. Exaggeration.

JAMES: Is this just all a big act for you?

H.R.: Absolutely!!! When I go on that stage, I'm not bad at all, but I have to pretend, you know. You've got to pretend to be somebody. Just like in wrestling.

JAMES: Do you pretend to be H.R.?

H.R.: As a matter of fact, yes!

JAMES: Well then, who are you really?

H.R.: Who am I truly? Well, actually I'm the King of England, but shhhhh, it's a secret!

JAMES: Is Paul Hudson still in there?

H.R.: I don't know, let's see. Where's my towel? Are you in there, Paul?

JAMES: So, when you're onstage, it's just an act?

H.R.: Oh, yeah. I'm acting, man. That's what Anthony Countey said: "You better go out there and entertain, and if you walk off that stage, we're through." I said, "No, it's not fair."

JAMES: Is it too much pressure sometimes?

H.R.: No. It's not too much pressure, but sometimes the girls are rather tempting, you know.

INTRODUCTION

I am a die-hard Bad Brains fan and have been since first lending my ears to their game-changing, self-titled, cassette-only debut album released on Reachout International Records in February 1982. The group's reputation had already ascended to legendary status in their adoptive home of New York City, where I, too, resided. In OG fan terms, I was late to the game; having first become aware of the Bad Brains and their incomparable vocalist and front man, H.R., a year after the ROIR release in 1983. I would not witness one of their renowned live gigs until the summer of 1985 at the newly launched, muggy-as-hell Jane Street Rock Hotel, when they "reunited" after a brief hiatus. I was unaware they'd ever left.

What I encountered that July evening on the west side of Manhattan was nothing short of life-altering. The Bad Brains were far and away the most intense band I'd ever seen, and the crowd matched their output with unbridled vehemence. Doc, Darryl and Earl played faster than fast, yet with a laser-like control only a seasoned musician might comprehend. H.R. was something else. You would swear he moved at a different speed than other human beings. His control of that room of punks, skinheads and curious onlookers—sometimes without uttering a single word—was unprecedented. The kids moved as he moved. They took a breather only when he did. They, myself included, bought into anything and everything he commanded. I became immediately convinced that there would never be a better band, nor a greater front man. I still believe that.

Aggressive music has always been a liberator for me; however, hard tunes with no soul quickly wear thin. H.R. exhibited soul where it could not be found previously. His lyrics contributed an urgency fueled by spirituality and a call to social justice, which substantiated the ferocity of the Bad Brains' earth-shattering soundscapes. This included the instances when Bad Brains broke it down to a mesmerizing, skank-drenched reggae rhythm. H.R.'s vocal style was otherworldly; ever vacillating between combative and graceful expression; all the while thrusting forth a righteous dose of rebellion served with a side of hope.

In 1989, seven years after that ROIR cassette dropped, I was afforded the honor and privilege of releasing said Bad Brains album on compact disc for the first time ever via the In-Effect Records label I cofounded. Our parent company, Important Record Distributors, already distributed the ROIR label in America, so we were able to reach an agreement to do so, as they were only interested in putting forth cassettes. We sold nearly twenty thousand of those CDs in the first six weeks, a watershed accomplishment for hardcore at the time.

My only direct interaction with H.R. up until that point had been tagging along with a journalist friend on his mission to interview H.R. prior to a gig on Long Island. After much scrutiny as to where the interview should take place— the tour bus was too cold, backstage was too noisy—H.R. concluded that the discussion should take place a few hundred yards beyond the parking lot of the venue, beneath a large bush. I thought it odd. To H.R., it seemed normal.

The intellection of materializing a book concerning H.R.'s life and career seemed well beyond possibility. This is H.R. after all. You've heard the stories: he's out of his mind; he's not all there; he only cares about Rasta. I wasn't quite sure what to think or believe. As daunting an undertaking as this biography seemed, I convinced myself to access anything and everything within my power to bring it to life. I mean, this is H.R. after all! Beginning from scratch was an intimidating suggestion. No one, myself included, could tell if H.R. was willing or able to participate in such a venture, given his recent history of uneven behavior. I recalled that a filmmaker based in Baltimore named James Lathos had begun work on a documentary film designed to convey H.R.'s story, so I obtained his number and cold-called him to see if he might be willing to work together on a book adaptation alongside his movie. James's response was warm and welcoming, and we decided to team up in an effort to do justice to H.R.'s personal narrative: James utilizing a camera and me with a pen, so to speak, all with H.R.'s full support and cooperation, which James had already secured.

By this point in late 2014, James had conducted countless hours of interviews with those close to H.R. both personally and professionally, in addition to folks who have been touched or moved by him from afar. Furthermore, dozens of hours were spent talking with H.R. himself over the course of several years, much of which while he was in the throes of debilitating mental illness, which had not yet been properly diagnosed. His erratic, frequently unsettling comportment had long since grown to mythic proportions. By the late eighties, Bad Brains supporters and admirers of H.R.'s reggae offerings with his group Human Rights alike had grown increasingly confused, disheartened and even disturbed by what appeared to the naked eye to be apathetic, detached live performances. Very few people knew, H.R. was suffering from a condition much more problematic than fans could have imagined.

Some of the results of the interviews with H.R. executed for this project are laborious and disconcerting, while others are free-flowing and on point. At times, he appeared to be disinterested in the discussions, while at other times, thoroughly engaged and engaging. I truly wanted this to be HIS book, with the story told only by H.R. Nevertheless, it was clear that additional voices were required to convey the saga, hence the oral history format for *Finding Joseph I*; the title comes from James Lathos literally finding H.R. residing in a squat in Baltimore a few years prior while seeking to interview him for a skateboard magazine.

Regardless, you will come to know and understand this passionate, gifted and distinctively complex artist and messenger a whole lot better through his words, as well as those of H.R.'s contemporaries and enthusiasts.

-Howie Abrams

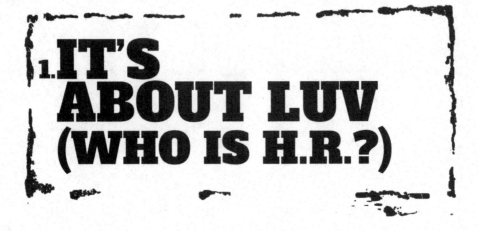

1. IT'S ABOUT LUV (WHO IS H.R.?)

NORWOOD FISHER | FISHBONE

H.R. is the genius madman musical prophet that has descended from planet . . . I don't know what. In a historical sense, he is the beginning of so much. It's hard to encapsulate the vastness of the influence, the energy and explosiveness. H.R.'s doing backflips and walking on the crowd like Jesus walking on water. He's an icon. He's choosing all the right notes to actually twist your heartstrings and bring this certain kind of tension and beauty, and there is no one like him.

CHINO MORENO | DEFTONES

He's the best vocalist ever as far as I'm concerned. When I first saw him performing, I was just blown away as far as the passion he had as a singer and as a human being. When I met him, I was perplexed by who he was. He's definitely his own being. What's behind what he does is a mystery to me, and that's intriguing. It makes it more interesting. I've met him a lot of different times over the decades and seen him in a lot of different places and in different moods. He can be the nicest, kindest man in the world, and he can be out there sometimes.

VERNON REID | LIVING COLOUR

He's the voice of one of the greatest American rock and roll bands of all time. H.R.'s one of the most contradicting, maddening, inscrutable, mysterious, dangerous . . . he's the real thing. He's what people talk about when they talk about danger in rock and roll. He's put people in the hospital. He's done that! That's a fact. He's dangerous like Lead Belly's dangerous, and he's also an incredibly sweet person. He's a living, walking contradiction.

KENNY DREAD | HUMAN RIGHTS

We're talking about a performer who took the total rage and boundary-breaking of rock and roll, and the deep spirituality of Rasta reggae and molded it into one. They have a saying in classical music: "Once in a hundred years." It's a once-in-a-hundred-years personality, a once-in-a-hundred-years energy. The pure shamanistic quality of pulling the energy in and smashing it back out again. H.R.'s voice: it's like a journey of emotional expression, and it's the sound of spirit. I'd never heard singing that had such nuances of expression. A tiny bit of a Southern accent, a tiny bit of African-American, a tiny bit of Jamaican accent. Snarls, yelps, screams. Nobody had ever done anything like that before.

JOHN JOSEPH | CRO-MAGS

If you listen to "Rastaman Chant" by Bob Marley where he's yodeling, H.R. was able to do incredible things with his voice, too, while putting out the most energetic performance you've ever seen in your life. Still, to this day, I bow down. I've seen all the bands in the early '70s. I was thirteen, fourteen, going to Madison Square Garden to see Led Zeppelin and The Who. I've never seen a front man better than H.R., and I don't think I ever will. Fishbone, Rage Against the Machine, Red Hot Chili Peppers . . . nobody can touch H.R. They can't even hold his chalice. It wasn't just the physical; it was the spiritual, too. That's where the real energy comes from, the soul, and he traveled with such a conviction and spirituality to his beliefs. He lived it. He wasn't talking shit. He was getting up every day, meditating and reading the Bible and Yahweh, living the life Ital.[2] He touched so many lives that went on to do amazing things. The way he delivered that message . . . you have the music, but if you don't have that front man that can deliver it and kill it on stage, you don't have the whole package. Bad Brains had the whole package primarily because of H.R.

RAKAA IRISCIENCE | DILATED PEOPLES

Imagine if James Brown and Bob Marley got together to freestyle at a punk rock show after watching acrobatics and gymnastics. You hear about hybrid music. You hear about fusion music, but you don't often hear about anybody who can do it for real. He does it all to the highest degree. There are a lot of people who are brave and don't mind pushing the envelope a little bit, but someone like H.R. doesn't have to rely on gimmicks or shtick of any sort. You're looking at genius. Going through some crazy hardcore punk, and you see people wilding out, and then all of a sudden breaking the whole crowd down in a way that's real. A lot of people don't have the skills to back up that attitude.

CHUCK TREECE | MCRAD, UNDERDOG

H.R. is like a modern-day Little Richard. Little Richard's focus back then was just basic rhythm and blues, and Richard was edgier than all of 'em: Prince and James Brown followed him, and a lot of people follow H.R. now. The closest reggae guy to H.R. is Eek-A-Mouse. You can compare Eek-A-Mouse's extravagances with H.R., but I don't think Eek-A-Mouse's voice would have worked over a hard band like Bad Brains. H.R. has a certain physical structure. If he turns it on, you're just freaked out. I think he's the only singer that can cut through the melody of a song and still make

---

[2] *Ital: food and living that Rastafarians view as vital in order to boost life energy*

sense. I think it comes from him understanding how to play guitar and understanding what songwriting is. If you have something to express . . . the hardest thing for a musician or a songwriter to do is just be expressive. You have to let go of the formulas. Most people won't take that risk because you have to embarrass yourself and sound different from the norm. He'll just do something totally drastic, way against the melody of a song, but it still applies. It's the weirdest thing.

RON ST. GERMAIN | PRODUCER

It's the H.R. signature. Nobody sounded like him or moved like him. The way he was running around, just firing on all cylinders, he was on his own little planet. You could not help but look at this guy and be engaged. Then he was also saying something. He was the king. Kind of the Bob Marley of that genre. To front that Bad Brains stuff, the amount of energy, and the amount of power and strength required for those vocals is staggering. He put himself into it 150 percent every time. Unreal, the things he's done with his voice. I mean, runs from the lows to the highs, the screams . . . unbelievable.

ANGELO MOORE | FISHBONE

He sings with melody even though he's singing with a lot of angst and edge. It has soul. It gives me another reason to sing punk rock with soul in it. Putting a lot of spiritual lyrics to his punk rock, which usually you don't get. Punk rock is normally about destruction. He makes it liberating. PMA: Positive Mental Attitude. That's another thing that stuck with me. Everybody should have it.

MICHAEL FRANTI | SPEARHEAD

Lyrically, all the songs were about things that were important to me. Things that were taking place in the world, social issues and human rights. As a young kid growing up in a suburban town and being one of the few black kids in my community who was really into skateboarding, and punk rock and hip-hop and all the rebellious things kids do at the time, to me, Bad Brains was the icon of my youth, and H.R was the leader.

M-1 | DEAD PREZ

What H.R. was writing for us was like a survival kit for the future. What happens when this shit breaks down? Where are your minds headed? That was the value of the music. Tomorrow's survival kit.

AL "JUDAH" WALKER | ZION TRAIN

He became a member of the 12 Tribes of Israel, which is a Rastafarian discipline. Rasta has four major disciplines, but all four of the disciplines have one thing in common and that's the faith that His Imperial Majesty Haile Selassie[3] is Yeshua [Christ] in his kingly character in revelation times, which is the time we are living in according to the Scriptures. That's when he became Ras Hailu—*Hailu* means power, and *Ras* means head. He ate, slept and drank music. It was like an energy source to reaffirm the spiritual things that he

---

[3]*Haile Selassie: the former emperor of Ethiopia*

deeply believed in. He was definitely a humanitarian, and a lot of injustices—not just in the music business but life in general—would tick him off. He had a militant spirit, and that militant spirit was his expression of being anti-Babylon and antiestablishment—another way to identify oneself as a rebel with a cause, not a terrorist or somebody destructive, but somebody that is expressing the opposite of what the system expects of us.

WILLIAM BANKS | H.R. BAND, ZION TRAIN

Every song has got something to do with a story. That's him. When he got busted on his son's birthday, he sang about it. When he got busted selling herb on Columbia Road, he sang about it on the next album. He called me up when he was doing one song for the Bad Brains and he was in jail. In the '80s, dreads wasn't no fashion. Back then, when you was dread,[4] you lived it.

ANTHONY COUNTEY | LONGTIME BAD BRAINS MANAGER

There were times that I thought H.R. was a healer. Kids would sometimes come to the show that were really sick. This kid came, I think it was in Arizona, and he had leukemia. He was really skinny and white as a sheet. He met H.R., and they talked for a long time. It was really intense. We came back a year later, and the kid was healed. The kid was fresh and strong. He was like, "Do you remember me?" H.R. was like, "Of course, I remember you." If nothing else, that capability of having respect for somebody who was in front of you at any given moment, and being in that moment with them and being honest and treating them like your brother. He took everything seriously. Lovingly but seriously.

ERIC WILSON | SUBLIME, LONG BEACH DUB ALLSTARS

I think he feels more comfortable onstage than anywhere else. Just from observing him in-between the bands when

---

[4] *Dread: a person with dreadlocks*

he's waiting to go onstage, he would just kind of sit behind the speakers and chill. He looks at ease when he's in front of people playing.

VERNON REID

We're watching a show and he's doing a song and he does a backflip and lands exactly at the end of the song, and it was like, "Game over!" I remember Corey being in the audience, and we looked at each other like, *WHAT THE FUCK?!* The only other person that I've seen do that was Nils Lofgren, 'cause Nils was a gymnast, but Nils used a little trampoline and he would run to the back of the stage and do a thing and *boom*, land—and it was incredible. H.R. did a standing somersault, which is one of the most difficult things. No run up. Standing. *Boom!* The only thing to compare it to was James Brown, the hardest working man in showbiz. Someone that can move like that changes the physical dimensions of the room, changes everything. H.R. would change the gravity of the room. He would do something and the audience would boil.

CHINO MORENO

When H.R. performs, he definitely transcends. He's somewhere else. It's not staged at all and that's what feels good about it. There's no inhibition. He's just in the music. The first time I ever saw him perform was with H.R., the group. It was probably one of the most intense shows that I've seen. It wasn't like he was jumping around and doing flips or anything. He was just standing there singing with his eyes closed and his head back, completely lost in the music. It's very honest, the way he lives. He is who he portrays himself to be. When you listen to records, you want to imagine what you're hearing is true and what they are talking about is real. He's a nomad, I guess, and I know there are many opportunities he's had to do this or to do that, and it seems to me that if he wanted to, that's what he'd be doing. He's just gonna do what he wants to do and you respect him for that.

COREY GLOVER | LIVING COLOUR

Every performer who speaks directly from themselves and is dealing with their internal mechanism and pushing it out, something takes over—and sometimes that's a very powerful presence. It's subconscious. It's guttural and raw and filled with every emotion you can think of. From extreme love to extreme hate; it's all mashed together and it pushes itself out. When you get to that place, when you achieve that, magic happens. H.R.'s in touch with that. You may not get it from him everyday, but onstage you know he's there. When you talk to him on the outside when he's not playing, he's very calm, very quiet. You can feel him thinking. It's a weird sense to feel someone thinking constantly. His mind is churning, his mind is moving. To feel that from somebody is a powerful thing.

ILL BILL | NON PHIXION, LA COKA NOSTRA, HEAVY METAL KINGS

It's a mixed bag what you're going to get with H.R., depending on what day of the week it is. When they say a person is like a flip of the coin, *he* really is. And that's what makes him who he is. I think H.R. is an uncontrollable substance. His gift is a gift *and* a curse. He's so over-the-top and unrestrainable; it's like everything that's held him back a little bit also makes him who he is, so you can't really have one side without the other. He's trying to balance his own inner scale and maintain that balance. I would never pass judgment on him 'cause I think we all go through that in life. We all have our inner demons and our internal battles and conflicts. H.R. is a perfect example of that. He's a testament to staying true to yourself as an artist, while at the same time, he's almost too real for his own good.

NICK HEXUM | 311

It must have been around the recording of one of our albums with Ron St. Germain in the early 2000s. We heard that H.R. wanted to come over and record some songs in our studio, and we were like, "Of course." It's just H.R. with an acoustic guitar doing the most beautiful songs that I'd ever heard and never heard again. I think H.R. wanted to have them recorded just to have them recorded. I don't think he put them out or anything. But first he said, "I think we should take care of the money," and he gets out a blank receipt book and pencil. He fills out what basically looks like a personal check with some ridiculous number of dollars on it, and he's like, "Okay, there you go. Now that we got that taken care of, we can record." Totally straight-faced, then he goes in there and records the most beautiful music I'd ever heard him do. I guess he has a different understanding of money than the rest of us, and that's a nice place to be.

MARK ANDERSEN | POSITIVE FORCE DC

H.R. is a bunch of different people. He is somebody who represents a whole lot more than maybe it's fair to ask anyone to carry on his shoulders. There's the Joseph who, onstage, is an absolute shaman. I mean, at his best, he is one of the most magnetic, electrifying, absolutely inspirational figures you will ever encounter. There is no front man better than Joseph at his best. No one. And most of the people that are big stars can't touch him—not at all. They don't even come close. So there's that Joseph. Then there's the Joseph that you know in personal life that is just extraordinarily generous, kind, thoughtful, and very very soft spoken. The kind of person that you would just want for your best friend. It's this other Joseph that was absolutely encouraging and supportive of young punks like Ian MacKaye and Henry Rollins and all these other folks in the early DC scene. Just an extraordinary, gentle soul. Then there's the Joseph that walks in darkness, who's utterly lost and apparently not willing to ask for help, and the contrast is heartbreaking. It's not that he's one of these three, he's *all* three. And that, for a lot of people—especially those of us who love him, who revere him as one of our main inspirations—it's a hard contradiction to navigate.

JIMMY GESTAPO | MURPHY'S LAW

I remember seeing Bad Brains at Irving Plaza when they were playing as Soul Brains in the late nineties and just being like, "Wow, what the hell happened to H.R.? What's wrong with him?" A lot of people in the hardcore community lose it. But with him, something's completely different. I don't know where he went, but something slipped and it just wasn't him anymore.

SONNY SANDOVAL | P.O.D.

I've heard everything from "It's just H.R. being H.R" to "H.R.'s out of his mind." I've heard "He's crazy" and also "He's not crazy; it's all just an act." I've heard it all. Like, "Yo, H.R., he's not all there." And "He's just high" or "He's pulling a trick on everybody." I think there is a fine line between genius and insanity. That is the mystique. Nobody knows what's up.

ALEC MACKAYE | UNTOUCHABLES, THE FAITH, IGNITION

It was the late '80s. I was working at 9:30 Club, and I hadn't seen the Bad Brains in a really long time, as people or a band or anything. And I just felt this desire to tell H.R. as a friend how much he meant to me. What he had done musically and philosophically and how much it meant to me. I was afraid I might not see him again for a long time or maybe ever. I remember being in the dressing room. I was with my brother, and I saw H.R. I said, "I just have to tell you that you've really changed me. I owe you a great debt for changing my life when I was younger. While I had the chance, I wanted to tell you that." At that moment, we had been talking pretty regularly and just having a conversation. When I said that, he got this look where he just went and he looked off beyond me and didn't say anything. Then I asked him a question and he didn't respond. He actually didn't talk to me at all for the rest of the night. That was the end of that, and I just walked away. Like, what was that about? My brother was like, "I don't know, man." I thought he was thinking about what I was saying, but I don't know.

AL "JUDAH" WALKER

I heard about an incident with him hitting somebody with a mic stand. That's when I knew, *No, that's not the Joe that I know. The Joe that I know wouldn't hit anyone with a mic stand for no reason.* Then I heard that he did it because somebody spit on him. The rest of the band members, they never saw anybody spitting on him. The H.R. that I remember might not be here now, but he's in there somewhere. For those who have written him off as crazy or a devil, I would never classify him that way, and I think that they need to rethink that. They should have empathy and understand that mental illness is not something anybody can control. It's not like you can control it, but I pray for him every day. I think about him all the time.

LORI CARNS HUDSON | H.R.'S WIFE

I recognized right away that there was some psychiatric issue. It was obvious to me, and I didn't know if anyone had tried to help him with that before. Most people would not really admit that there was something wrong. I don't even like to use the word "wrong." I think it's just different. People would say, "Oh, he's just eccentric. He's just being a rock star," and I said, "You guys are not facing reality." He really needs some help, but it was partly him being resistant to that. That was a big part of it. I know that there are other people in his life who had tried before to get him to see a doctor, and he just wouldn't.

NORWOOD FISHER

I've heard stories about things that happened along the course of Bad Brains' history. What might be looked at like self-sabotage. On another level, what was punk rock about again? It was about rebelling and not becoming part of the status quo. So on one hand, somebody's waving a lot of money and everybody needs to eat, and I could dig it, but on the other hand, there's a punk rock ethic and H.R. is standing his ground, going, "I don't want to go down that path." I can understand maybe the frustration of the other band members at those moments when it was, like, right there. So as a fan, yes, I'm disappointed they didn't get those opportunities to be a popular band. They didn't get to take advantage. If it was H.R. sabotaging it, as the stories go, there's some disappointment, but there's some understanding, too. For one, it might be the punk rock ethic. Otherwise, that's the pitfalls of rolling with a madman.

EARL HUDSON | BAD BRAINS, HUMAN RIGHTS,
             H.R.'S BROTHER

He's a carefree spirit, but you have to come to a realization that you can't live your life carefree or you won't have a roof over your head. That's how stuff is run, how things come about. You have to work, and you have to care. I guess he's fighting that now, but you have to come to a realization that that's how things are. Because you can only lead people down a path so far. Everybody needs somebody, and no man is an island, and so on. But that's a personal thing, and everybody struggles with that within themselves and with God. That's how that is.

QUESTLOVE | THE ROOTS

H.R is the person through whom I vicariously express my rage. More often than not, I grab early Bad Brains material to relieve the stress and the anger I feel. I can channel it through his music. Maybe he was an unwilling leader of a movement. Regardless, there was a movement that changed a lot of young fans. Still to this day, they look to him for inspiration, it's an each-one, teach-one society. Stuff he did thirty years ago is still being discovered today. It will never die or be disposable. That's a sign of true art. It's as if he is a silent ninja. I've never seen anyone that charismatic or that in command of their performance. That's the type of experience you see in older artists of Prince's stature or James Brown's stature or Michael Jackson's stature. That confidence that puts them at that level. I know the thing that makes him H.R. is the fact that he just rebels against the system. I've heard billions of H.R. stories, but I just wonder what would have happened if certain decisions that he made in his personal life and his professional life were made so he could have made it to that level of success.

COREY GLOVER

To me, he is channeling something more raw and powerful than any of us could ever imagine. Just to be a fly on the

wall of his mind would be . . . I don't think I could take it. I don't think any of us could take it. To this day I try to understand it. Every time I see Joseph it's like, wow. All of us aspire to be that dude, and he got it and always had it. As a singer, I say this all the time, all I'm doing is a cheap imitation of H.R. For real. A real cheap imitation.

WILLIAM BANKS

Some people think about the market and some people don't. H.R. is type of person that don't think about a market. H.R. is just straight up true to what he is. He lived the life of a rocker, a hardcore punk and he's still doin' it, and people don't understand. He's not living in a fancy house. He's not driving no fancy car. He's H.R., Human Rights, and he's living his story.

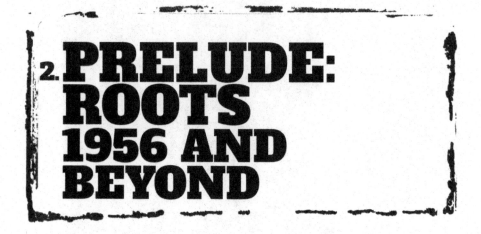

2. PRELUDE: ROOTS 1956 AND BEYOND

When I was born, my mom didn't see me for three days because I had pneumonia. She said that after the third day, she gave me her hand; I grabbed her one little finger and I stopped crying. After that everything was all right.

-H.R.

H.R.

I was born on Feb 11, 1956 and my parents gave me the name Paul Denard Hudson. I came from a great childhood, great background, great family. I was born in England and later relocated to DC. I did spend a little bit of time in Jamaica, Texas, Alabama, New York, and from there we went to Washington, DC. We did stop in California, and we were in Waianae, Hawaii, too. My father, Leon, was in the Air Force, and my mother, Carmen, was a nurse. She has a beautiful face. My mother and father . . . both of them are so top ranking. They're still together after all these years.

EARL HUDSON

My mom's from Jamaica, and my dad's from Alabama. My dad met my mother while stationed in England, and Joseph was born in Liverpool. My father then relocated from England, taking my mother with him to America. They had me when they came back to the States.

H.R.

I remember as a child living in Jamaica . . . it was there that I heard my first reggae song. Anyway, I was about three years old, and my mother dropped me and my brother off at my Auntie May's house in Kingston. My parents left and went on their way. They had to get some things together so that my mom could go to the US. I remember I closed my eyes and I said to myself, "I'm not going to open them up until my mom returns." There was one thing that I needed, and that was my mother. It's good to have your father, but you need to have your mother, too. I wanted to stay in Jamaica and my mother said, "Okay, you want to stay? I'm leaving you then, and I'll come back another day." I thought she was just joking around. She didn't come back for almost a year, when she got the paperwork together to go to America with my father.

EARL HUDSON

We did some schooling in Jamaica, and I remember the teacher hit my ass on the hand with a ruler for some reason or another. We were little kids. So long ago. We didn't spend that much time growing up there. Later, my father was stationed in Hawaii. We were there for four years. It was crucial. We learned to skateboard way before all these prominent cats that are big skaters now. Skateboarding and sand-surfing on the beach. That was a real cool childhood. Me and Joe both really liked to swim in Hawaii. There's a story about my dad saving his life one time when we were kids. H.R. swam out too far and couldn't get back. The current was taking him out, man.

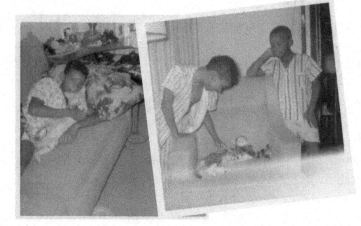

H.R.

My dad was sitting on the beach, just watching his two sons having fun in the ocean. I saw a little boat that was docked maybe a hundred yards away from the shore. I was thinking I would swim all the way there, so I took off for the boat. I could swim underwater real good, but on top, I wasn't really swimming good yet. About halfway to where the boat was docked, I had to come up for air, and there was nothing to stand on. I was yelling, "Help, help!" So my dad threw down his cigarettes from out of his pocket and jumped in the water with his clothes on to rescue me. He swam to me, grabbed me and then stood up in the water, and it was only about to his waist. But Hawaii was a beautiful place. It was an adventure every day.

Earl's been playing drums all his life. He had a little cardboard drum set, and one day, I was playing with him and smashed it on his head. He wanted a real drum set for Christmas, but my dad could not afford it at the time. After that, he got a snare drum, and we started a group called The Thunderbirds. There was a brother named Jeff who played guitar, and another brother named Jimmy who played guitar. We'd take the boxes and set them all up. I had my little ukulele because I couldn't afford no electric guitar, but we would do shows in the back yard for the kids in the neighborhood.

We used to play The Beatles' "Help" and "I Want To Hold Your Hand," and the other song we did was the *Batman* theme: *duh na nuh na nuh na nuh na nuh na—Batman*. That's how it started for us. Then in the fifth grade, Earl got his first authentic set of drums, but still for him it was not enough. He wanted the kind he had seen on television that Ringo Starr had. My father was saying, "Come on, Earl, give me a break. You want me to buy you a $10,000 set of drums and you're only in the fifth grade?" He stood up and looked at Earl, put his fist in the air and said, "Boy, are you crazy?!"

EARL HUDSON

We came back to the mainland, and after some time in California, we moved in with my grandparents in Alabama while my dad was stationed overseas. We lived in Texas, too—in Abilene for a couple of years—and he was on the football team.

H.R.

I joined the football team in the eighth grade. Everybody was taller than me and big and strong. I had my little helmet and my pads. One day we played in a tournament in Texas, and my teammates said, "We're going to call you 'The Gnat' because you seem to be able to squeeze in and out of things and you're fast." On defense, I would work as one of the cornerbacks. One time I had an interception and kept on running; one of them dudes hit me, and I got demolished, man. I just walked off the field and said, "That's it. I don't want to be no football player no more." From there, though, we had several places we moved to. We were always on the move. I must have gone to about eleven, twelve, thirteen different schools in my life.

EARL HUDSON

Joe was a serious athlete, man. He was a pole vaulter and track star in school. A serious diver too. He ran hurdles and got a letter in pole vaulting. We were in Queens, New York, for a little bit, where he was on the swim team. The coach wanted him to stay because he wanted him to try to make the Olympic team, but my mom said, "No." Pretty sure she knew we were going to move. My dad decided to move us to the DC/Maryland area. That's when he retired out of the Air Force. He went to work with Boeing Aviation as a mechanic 'cause that's what he was doing in the Air Force.

H.R.

Boy, that was a trip for me because it was my first time actually being away from government children and I wasn't around service people. I spoke differently, I looked different and I did not do what those kids did in DC. As a youngster I was withdrawn. I didn't talk to people at all. I went to Central High School off of Addison Road, Central Avenue, around 1971 or '72. Then in 1973, we relocated again, and I began attending my classes over at Potomac High School. I graduated from Potomac the following year. I wanted to play music, but I was encouraged to become a doctor or a lawyer, or something that would allow me to utilize my talents in a professional way, and at the same time have a consistent paying job. So staying in school was mandatory, a priority. At that time, I really didn't understand why—but now I do.

MARK ANDERSEN

After high school, I think it's fair to say H.R.'s parents had concerns that he didn't have a direction. He started drifting. He was doing security work, going out with girls—as teenagers do—dabbling in drugs. He found himself in a situation where he was getting addicted to heroin and had gotten a girl pregnant. He was a gifted person working a security job. No offense to security folks, but clearly, he had a whole lot more potential, and his father—who was an extraordinary figure in his life, a very strong affirmative and present figure—was getting pretty disgusted with him. He's becoming a dad and working as a security guard. He was essentially plotting to go into pre-med. He was going to study to be a doctor. I think that was the hope of his family, but it just wasn't working for him. And at the same time, he started to drift into drugs. He was on the edge of the abyss.

H.R.

My brother was more into the scholastics. A lot of my focus was on girls at that time. I was heavy into the babe scene. I had met a sister named Joanne and another sister by the name of Karen. They used to talk to me about their experiences in school with the teachers and other boys. I would run up the phone bill, and my dad would say, "Put that phone down! What are you doing? Where are you going?" I would be off looking for those girls.

3. MAKE A JOYFUL NOISE 1971–1977

By the second grade I had a knack for writing poems and songs. It's an amazing gift that God gave me.

-H.R.

ALVAREZ TOLSEN | CHILDHOOD FRIEND

I first met Earl when I was a junior in high school. We moved from Northeast DC to Maryland in '71. I'd never been on a school bus in my life, and when I came out of school the first day, I saw the buses but didn't know which one was mine. I heard somebody say, "This one over here," and it was Earl. We became buddies. One night H.R. and Earl's mother and father were going out, so they had a party. Earl said, "My brother's having a party, so come on over." We started hanging out, and I saw H.R. with a couple girls. He started playing Earth, Wind & Fire, and I was like, "I didn't know your brother was into Earth, Wind & Fire." They were a big group back then, and we used to go see them at the Capital Centre. Back then I was like a bootlegger. I had a lot of wine; so when I came, the word spread throughout the apartments. H.R. caught wind of it and said, "Hey man, I heard you got some of this wine." I said, "Yeah." So I go and get a bottle and brought that over, and it was a great party. H.R. was no different than the next person as far as I was concerned. He was just Earl's brother.

MARLANDO TOLSEN | CHILDHOOD FRIEND

We would go swimming at night, and that guy . . . his mind was beyond the time. We would take LSD, and I'm tripping, watching this guy on a diving board and he goes up in the air about fifteen feet and does a triple somersault off a diving board into an eight–and–a–half–foot pool. I'm thinking, *This guy is unbelievable!*

EARL HUDSON

Alvarez was one of my best friends. I'd go over his house, and we'd listen to music a lot. We were always messing around with different instruments, but Gary (Miller) used to be in junior high school with me and we used to be in the same classes. Gary was always in a band playing bass, and I introduced him to H.R. We were always going to some of Gary's gigs and then just hanging out or whatever. I think Joe wanted to learn an instrument, so Gary started to teach him a little bit about the guitar. We were determined. We wanted to try to start a band.

H.R.

Addison Road, that's where I first met Gary and Darryl. I heard them jamming out over at our friends Marlando and Alvarez's house. One day I heard them playing some music in this basement, and I said, "Oh, are you all going to be in a band together?" They said, "Yeah. That's right, man." We just started to play all kinds of music all day long. I didn't really know if the music we were playing was going to be popular or not, but it didn't matter because we were just having fun imitating the guys that we would see on television like Jimi Hendrix, Paul Revere and the Raiders, and the Rolling Stones.

ALVAREZ TOLSEN

My mother would go out, and Earl would come over with his drums. You couldn't play music in the apartments because the apartment people would complain, so they would come over to our house because nobody could hear us. I would play guitar, and then H.R. started playing the kalimba.[5] This became a weekend thing. Then summer broke, and things started forming into a group. Earl would come over and play the drums. H.R. with the kalimba, and some other guy—I can't think of his name—would play congas. And then you'd see other musicians start to come. H.R. would bring people he knew, and all of a sudden, there's Gary Miller. I knew Darryl. He did not know them back then. Darryl would come along with his guitar to collaborate. To make a long story short, H and Earl moved out to Oxon Hill. Their mother and father got a house over there, and they started having parties and inviting us over. That's when the music really started flowing. We were doing Friday parties and charging people fifty cents to get in. It was just a jam session. One night it was me, H.R. and Gary, and we didn't go over so great with the crowd, because we were charging fifty cents and we were not together. H.R. didn't play the bass real good, and people started to get annoyed. They would say, "This motherfucker can't play bass worth a shit." So Darryl happened to be outside. I go find him, and he wouldn't come in and play that bass for some reason. The next day—I don't know how it happened, he called them or H.R. called him—but they started doing the Mind Power group. That was progressive jazz: Chick Corea, Stanley Clarke and all them seems to be . . . *Return to Forever.* They started doing covers, but I don't think that lasted too long

---

[5]*Kalimba: a type of African musical instrument*

because the neighborhood didn't like that kind of music. *RTF* was way before its time, and they didn't understand Stanley Clarke and them back then. Around here, we were with Parliament Funkadelic, Graham Central Station types, you know . . . Motown. People were just scratching their heads like, *What's goin' on?*

H.R.

Another group I was bumping into in those days was Mandrill. We decided to go check them out when they were doing a concert over at the Capital Centre. They were so colorful and original in their style and techniques—their clothing and conscious level of speaking. We drove home that night, and the next day we were trying to play some of their songs. It was pretty cool but kind of comical, though. Darryl and Gary couldn't make up their minds what instruments to play. Sometimes Darryl would want to play the bass, so he gave his guitar to Gary, and Gary gave Darryl the bass. To our surprise, word got out that we were playing, so we were requested by some of the kids in school to do shows. We wanted to practice first and perfect our ideas. Everything just had to be perfect. We tried the same song about one hundred times and finally it started making sense.

EARL HUDSON

Joe would be in our room adamantly studying, rehearsing, practicing until he got it right. Him and Gary were actually going to go to college. They were pre-med and were gonna try and be doctors, but we were always listening to music and going to concerts, so we decided we wanted to go the musical route—and that's what we did.

ALVAREZ TOLSEN

H.R. was the kind of guy who was never satisfied with himself. He had something inside of him that he wanted to do when he came up with the music. That's when he found himself. I could see a light in him. He became a whole different person. There was always something on his mind: *I'm not using my full potential. I don't wanna be a pawn for anybody. I wanna be myself and go out and make my own name.* And he did that writing songs.

MARLANDO TOLSEN

He had this job at a hospital. He was a security guard, and he was really depressed. I said, "Hey, man, you're depressed?" He had a brand-new Camaro, a fast car, and *he's* depressed? It just wasn't enough for him. He said, "I got something in me that I can't explain." You could see he was really depressed at work. He said, "We're gonna form a group," so they formed Mind Power. They had a gig over at the house off Southern Ave. The band didn't play well that night. They flopped. I came outside afterward. He's holding onto this lamppost and I'm like, "Darryl, what's up?" He said, "I can't believe we failed." I said, "No, that's just the beginning. Everybody bombs. Just got to keep at it."

MARK ANDERSEN

Paul Hudson was a really gifted kid. It was obvious he was a very good athlete, too. He was very sharp but not always willing to put in the effort to do as well academically as he could. As I recall, his father came home one day and found his gifted son lying on the couch when there were clearly many things to do. One thing led to another, and they were sitting there in an argument. All of a sudden, his dad basically says, "Why don't you go do something with your life? Just do something like read a book." And as people do in these kinds of arguments, Paul jumped up and said, "I will. I will read a book," and he goes over and just grabs a book off the shelf without even looking. They're his father's books, and he pulls out *Think and Grow Rich* by Napoleon Hill, which is arguably the fountainhead where all of the self-help, positive thinking books come from. It predates Norman Vincent Peale's *The Power of Positive Thinking* and was followed up by *Success Through a Positive Mental Attitude.*

H.R.

Positive Mental Attitude: no matter what you've got to do in life, be positive. Keep a burning desire. Keep the truth going. It was possible, but one would have to be patient and determined and also love what he did. I saw that a lot of things discussed in the book I was going through. I decided to apply those teachings and instructions to my everyday living.

EARL HUDSON

"Whatever your mind can conceive and believe, your mind can achieve." The philosophy in essence was really about God, but there was also this thing where you have to make a plan and visualize the plan. But if you don't stick to this plan, within five years you can pretty much fuck yourself. It was all about keeping a Positive Mental Attitude. You have

to focus on your plan and try not to differ from that. Be focused and no other thing can interrupt that, or should interrupt that.

MARK ANDERSEN

Joseph read the book, and by all accounts, it absolutely altered the direction of his life. *Think and Grow Rich* . . . you think, *Oh well, it's some sort of goofy get-rich thing.* Well, yeah, but it's also a spiritual book, talking about how people live their lives. Not so much different than something like *The Purpose Driven Life* by Rick Warren now. The idea being you have to have a reason to be here and without that purpose to focus on, you're gonna be lost. And whether you want a revolution, or you just want to make a good living, it all starts with that can-do attitude. That hit Joseph so hard that he actually started becoming kind of an ambassador for it. He took it around. First his brother read the book, and then some of his friends, including Sid McCray and Gary Miller and Darryl Jenifer. They all read the book. They all started messing around in a little band that turned into something called Mind Power, the name coming straight out of the book. They were essentially a jazz/fusion group inspired by *Return to Forever.* They began to use the concepts from Napoleon Hill's book in their music in the same way that *Return to Forever* used spiritual concepts from other sources.

4. ROCK FOR LIGHT 1977–1979

I think the philosophy was to have something positive to say—have some kind of prophetic message that would prove to people that we could do something better.

-H.R.

MARK ANDERSEN

Mind Power didn't really take off. They were trying to do a jazz fusion thing with a few other things thrown in. Everybody seems to remember the first and only Mind Power gig as pretty much a disaster. After that, Paul kind of withdrew and was questioning his path like, *Is this really going to work out?* He's feeling like, *Oh, my God, I have another thing I'm failing at.* One day, Darryl brought the band over to see their friend Sid McCray. The Sid Paul had known previously as just an average kid from PG County was gone. He had become this crazy punk rocker, all dressed up in chains and spikes and leather jackets and torn jeans and all of that.

SID MCCRAY | FRIEND

When I first met H.R., he was trying to find something, just like I was trying to find something when I found punk rock. I was watching a documentary on PBS, and they were showcasing the Sex Pistols and The Damned and all that. Me and Darryl, we had been messing around with some funk and go-go and all kinds of stuff back in that era. This shit comes on the TV with all this energy, and I just tore my room up! I heard this one song and just ripped the whole house apart. I told H.R., "You've got to check this shit out, man." And he was like, "Man, fuck you. What the fuck is this shit?" So the Mind Power guys come over. They needed a new direction. I guess the jazz thing wasn't happening. So I'm looking out the window, and they come walking up looking like the Beatles on the *Abbey Road* album. There's H.R. with his big KISS boots, Earl with his little outfit on and Doc was like the conservative 'hood guy and shit, at least for back in the day.

EARL HUDSON

We were into all this progressive jazz, *Return to Forever* and Weather Report and cats like that. They had been playing really adamantly and fast, and that was our shit back then. But after a while, those dudes started going commercial and started to lose the power behind the music. That's where Sid came in and introduced us to the punk rock. We were like, "Hell yeah, we want to do some of that stuff," so we started to play punk. We came up with our own shit.

JUAN DECOSTA | CHILDHOOD FRIEND

I met H.R. through a buddy of mine, Ray Watts. He would always tell me, "You gotta meet my boys." One day he said, "Let's go over there and see this muthafucka, Paul." I go over there and we get to talking, and we get to smoking a little weed. We was getting high and I was like, "I want to play some music for you." I played this muthafucka some Iggy Pop and this dude throws me out of his house! He said, "I don't want to hear that crazy shit." I said, "Get the fuck outta here." Three months later I go out to this house party and I see muthafuckin' Bad Brains. These muthafuckas got on leopard pants and they're turned-up like a muthafucka! I'm like, *Is this the same guy that threw me out of his house?!*

H.R.

Sid played us the Sex Pistols' *Never Mind the Bollocks* album. The band members were some of the most intriguing looking individuals I'd ever seen. They had black eyes and drool and mohawks and everything. Well, I listened to the music, and it was shocking. I guess you could call it awesome. It was outrageous. I asked Sid, "Where's the group now?" He said, "Well, they broke up." And then he played some Ramones for us, which I found absolutely incredible. They had this one song called "Rockaway Beach," and it was really cool. Also, we heard their song "Bad Brain," and we kinda clicked with that. We got our name from that. A few days later, I heard that the Ramones were going to be performing at the University of Maryland, and I had a chance to go. I could not believe it. The singer didn't move around much. He just kind of stood there, but buddy, the audience was just jumping all around. I said, "Oh boy, look at this! I want this!"

SID MCCRAY

I dug the PMA thing on a surface level, but I didn't really get into it. I was still into my destructive thing. I still had to run that course. I sung with the band for a little while, but I fizzled out because I saw H.R. was a much better singer. It wasn't a competition thing; I just thought he was a better singer, more theatrical. And at that time, they saw Bob Marley and I wasn't ready to see Bob Marley. I still had some running and tearin' things up to do, so we split ways.

JUAN DECOSTA

I always thought that Sid was going to be the man 'cause Sid was really the rockstar back then out of all of them. Joe's demeanor was a little quiet compared to Sid, but there was something about H.R. He had that muthafuckin' attitude.

H.R.

We went to see Bob Marley at the Capital Centre, and that was it for me. I was just floored. It's like the barrier . . . the walls, came tumbling down. My eyes were opened. I see all that hair, and I said, "No way! No way could an African have hair all the way down his back like that." Some big old dreads. I was way upstairs in the back, and I said, "Darryl, Gary, Earl . . . I'm goin' up front." So I was trying to, you know, "Pardon me, excuse me, pardon me," and I walked up to the front. It was a full house, and all the kids—elders, too—were wearing red, gold and green like one great big picnic. If you were inside the Capital Centre that night, you would have sworn the sun was shining. It felt like it was in the daylight. And the band played everything: jazz, rock and roll, funk and then some of the sweetest soul and reggae you ever heard in your life.

It reminded me of Stevie Wonder, but to the next level—like to the outer limits, in a way. Like Stevie Wonder after having four or five cups of mushroom tea.

WILLIAM BANKS

The punk rock scene came into play with the reggae scene. Don't forget, The Clash and them used to do reggae, too. So all these things go into H.R.'s mind. He really wanted to do the reggae for the peace and love and the vibe and the Jah thing, and then punk is on top of what he's saying. I used to call it "dirt rock" back then. It didn't have a scene or a title. That's just the sound that we wanted to hear.

H.R.

I would say both reggae and punk are rebelling against those who rebel against the authenticity of the essence of love. But I think even more important than that is the conviction behind the unity of the two. With reggae, kids felt united with that kind of music because it was the sincerity, the earnestness and, of course, the African struggle. Bob Marley sang of a life that would give hope, and even spoke of dreams coming true for certain brothers and sisters who might be looking for a better way of life, a better way of living. Whether they were black, white, yellow, red or brown; had long hair or short hair; wore glasses or didn't wear glasses; were skinny or fat. We wanted to be able to take hold of that during that time and actually become a vehicle or a chariot for our generation.

EARL HUDSON

It's a spiritual thing. When we were kids living in Jamaica, I remember while riding the bus, there was this cat on the sidewalk who had dreads—but we didn't know what that was about—but through God's affirmation, he led us into playing reggae music. It was just something that was meant to be, and that's what we ended up playing along with punk rock music.

MARK ANDERSEN

When H.R. first listened to the music that Sid was listening to, Darryl recalls that his reaction was, "This is madness. This is noise. What is this?" And Darryl was like, "No, you don't understand. There is something here, let me explain it to you," and he kind of broke it down for him. As H.R. recounted it, something in that moment caused something in the universe to slip into place for him. And all of a sudden, he turned to the others with a big smile and said, "Why don't we play some punk rock, y'all?"

That's the birth of Bad Brains. They took all of that experience—the African-American middle-class experience in a city that not long ago was a segregated city, within their lifetime—and they are taking these musical influences and the skills that they developed from trying to play this complicated jazz fusion, and they are adding in the incredible energy and antiestablishment fervor. That passion. That's punk rock. And what they created out of all of these pieces is something unprecedented. You can see its roots but it's something entirely new at the same time. I think it was the mastermind alliance Napoleon Hill suggested, the ideas of *Think and Grow Rich*: the PMA, the intense focus, which, to H.R., looked exactly like what he would conceive a band to be. Four individuals pulling together the power of their minds, their hearts and all of their skills towards one objective with intense dedication, focus and concentration. That is what created this incredible entity called Bad Brains.

IAN MACKAYE | MINOR THREAT, FUGAZI

The way I recall that we got into punk or whatever . . . there was new wave, and there was punk. New wavers had become identified as being really sort of goofy: The B 52's, Devo, that kind of stuff. When you said "punk," a lot of people would think Sid Vicious—junkie, nihilistic, self-destructive. We weren't like that, so we just said, "We're hardcore." Meaning: we didn't need to get dressed up and pretend to be tough because we were tough. That was our thing. We were kids making music 'cause we just didn't give a fuck about what other people thought. We knew we were not well-liked by the straight people or punks or new wave people. We just said, "Well, we don't care. This is our music, and we're just hardcore punks." That's how we started to use that term.

ALEC MACKAYE

When I found out what kind of music the Bad Brains started off listening to, the jazz fusion stuff, I was baffled by their decision. However, it told me that they saw punk rock as important and viable. Like a knife, they're going to cut through some bullshit, so they selected that. For a lot of us who were getting into punk rock at that time, it had to do with the fact that it was attainable and was something that we could do. They could have done anything they wanted to musically, within reason. They were talented musicians and had more sophisticated taste than some people, yet they picked punk rock. They trusted that vehicle. When I discovered that, it gave punk validation beyond just being "meathead music" that anybody could do.

MARK ANDERSEN

In the beginning, they grabbed onto this punk rock thing with extraordinary fervor, the same way they grabbed onto the Napoleon Hill stuff. There was a book by Caroline Coon called *1988*, which apparently they got a hold of and used to learn about the politics of the scene. I think they were particularly impacted by stories about The Clash, the way they went into the poorer areas of London and were in solidarity with the Jamaicans and other immigrants. How they melded reggae and punk rock together and were inspired and influenced by Bob Marley—who, of course, would become a huge inspiration for Joseph as well. That book became their template, and they took new names: Darryl became Darryl Cyanide, Gary became Dr. Know, Paul began to only use H.R. and I don't know if Earl took on a name or not, but they were all punked up. Folks like Ian MacKaye and Henry Rollins remember the first time they saw them handing out fliers at a Cramps show in Georgetown, and they were just amazed, like, "Who on earth are these guys?" These are the wildest-looking punk guys we've ever seen, and they're the only African-American folks there. The audacity, the vision and the courage of these guys was extraordinary. The spiky cuts, the ripped up jackets, the safety pins, the studs; all of this stuff was the initial approach of Bad Brains.

JUAN DECOSTA

Joe was sharp. He had his own style. He was different. It was sort of a little funky, British type of punk, rock and roll thing. It was so beyond its time back then. He was on the edge like a muthafucka back then. Joe was real comfortable in his skin. Back in them days, people were looking at him like, *Who is this weird dude? Is he gay? What type of trip is he on?* It never seemed to bother him. He just did not care, and I loved that about him. He just didn't care about what people thought.

ALEC MACKAYE

They would be driving down Wisconsin Avenue in Georgetown and H.R. was yelling at all these people in front of the Key Theatre in a British accent, "All of you are fucking poseurs!" That's the first time I actually saw them. They were just a completely new take on what punk rock meant to me at that point, and, I think, for everybody in DC.

EARL HUDSON

We had started rehearsing day and night. H.R. and Gary used to work at a bomb-making facility out in Virginia. Seriously, H.R. and Gary used to make bombs and missiles and shit, and I used to work at an electrical place. Darryl was going to electronics school, so after work, I'd go pick Darryl up at midnight or one in the morning, come back to the house and we'd rehearse until five in the morning or something like that. We did that for like a year straight and then started playing some shows. The first show was at our house. We had some kids come through there, and it was pretty cool. Then we started playing places like Madam's Organ. That was a coalition type of thing with a lot of hippie cats who were into music. Joe was staying out there in the Adams Morgan area.

ALEC MACKAYE

DC at that time, as far as major cities go, the infrastructure was not there, so there was a ton of crime. They never really recovered from the riots in '68. 14th Street was all fucked up and half the buildings were still empty. It was more industrial in those times. It was very divided and I think it's still pretty divided. Adams Morgan was much more marginal. In that neighborhood, if somebody wanted to go to McDonald's at 18th and Columbia, you would get like four guys to go. Just to go to a McDonald's that's only about four blocks away. A lot could happen in four blocks, particularly with the way we were looking at the time. And something always did happen. It was tough. But generally, that happens to also be where art happens and music like punk rock happens. Places that will tolerate it are places that tend to have this complexity.

RUSSELL BRAEN | MUSIC MANAGER, MADAM'S ORGAN

Back in the late '70s, Adams Morgan was boarded up. It was what they called "redlined," which meant that the banks weren't loaning any money to any of the property owners there, with the idea that the banks would slowly get control of those properties. Everybody knew it was going to become a great big something. It is a tourist trap now. I was there last night, and it's just insane. As the artists who were in that neighborhood, we worked our way out of that neighborhood by renovating those houses until we couldn't afford to live there anymore. It was rough.

H.R.

The Madam's Organ building is where we started. I lived in the apartment way up on the top floor. All the kids would group together out front where we would have little jam sessions. It was free to get in in those days, or you would give what you could afford—donations and contributions. They renovated the building, but in those days it was pretty run down. Also there were some Ethiopian restaurants. It was a post-riot neighborhood. The sixties riots came up in here, and most of the buildings were burned down or torn up. But through community effort and a lot of good-hearted people, little by little, they renovated the buildings and fixed them up—the landlords and the people from the community like us. They would have meetings every week, and people would put their two cents worth in and try and help out. It was more like an artist co-op in those days. Musicians ran it, musicians pulled it together and musicians would support musicians, artists, painters, sculptors, belly-dancers, rap artists, go-go artists and also brothers and sisters in the punk rock movement—or what we called in those days, "hardcore." There were a few reggae bands, too, but not many. A lot of good bands played Madam's Organ like S.O.A., Teen Idles, The Slickee Boys, D.O.A., and Trenchmouth.

ALEC MACKAYE

Everything was happening there. I have a huge amount of affection for the place now, and I see the gift of it. But at the time, it drove me nuts—half the shit that was going on in there. I wanted to have a punk rock revolution, and we put up with these old hippies because Madam's Organ was where you could play. There wasn't a real loving relationship at the time. They liked what we were doing, and we were putting up with them because they weren't banning us, calling the police or throwing us out. It was a safe place in that way. Just a total stoner hippy situation.

RUSSELL BRAEN

We never thought we would have so much history with the Bad Brains. We thought maybe they would play once or twice, but we ended up hitting it off really well. Partially because we were all wicked potheads and they were too. I remember after their first show, we had just harvested a bunch of ditch weed in West Virginia, and we were rolling these giant spliffs. We put towels under the doors of the room and I just remember seeing someone from the band leaning out the window of the house waving this baseball bat like, "Woo hoo." That sort of sealed the deal. We were good with those guys after that. When they played, they usually would set up and Dr. Know would make sure his guitar was going good, and then they would just sort of start into the first song. The place would just burst into activity, like this rioting mass of people. Super high energy, super emotional. I remember once H.R. played this song about the mother of his son, Simeon, who had broken up with him not long before I met the band. He played that song with his full heart, and I remember being in tears. I was sort of embarrassed, but once the song ended, I looked around to my left and my right, and everyone else in the room was just in tears, too. H.R. ended up after that song curled up in a fetal position, half under a chair on the stage. I will never have a concert moment like that again. You know, it's not one of the most famous songs or anything like that, but as far as the amount of raw emotion one man could put through a group of people, that was the highest I've ever seen in my life.

SKEETER THOMPSON | SCREAM

I don't wanna get too into his drug use, but he did drugs, and he'd be fucking girls in stairways and he had this outlook like, live fast and die young. He had a presence about him. He could get just about any girl at the time.

JUAN DECOSTA

Shit, everybody was getting high back then. You'd do a show; somebody would hit you off with something, then *boom!* The dude is performing, but it didn't take anything away from what he was doing on that stage. He might have been high, but that man was on point. In them Madam's Organ days, Bad Brains was already the greatest rock and roll band in the world.

RUSSELL BRAEN

Those early shows at Max's Kansas City, or CBGB and some of the Madam's Organ shows, he took a hit of acid before those shows and got pretty high. I think it probably helped him with the intensity and the motion that he liked to get into. I remember one day we were sitting on the rooftop and he told me that he was never going to take LSD again, that it wasn't right for his chosen religion. I totally respected that.

H.R.

It was there that I met Al Walker, and also Julian Cambridge, and [Ray] Chinna [Shim] and another brother named Naphtali. We would all meet there. I wasn't dread in those days, and they had hipped me to a lot of reggae and Rasta, and it was there that the group and I began to learn about the ways of I and I[6] people and Jah. They turned me onto a lot of different things, and I began to read my information. It is in this neighborhood that I began to learn about the authentic movement of the Rastafarians.

ALVAREZ TOLSEN

There were a lot of Rastas uptown on Columbia Road, and they used to come see shows at Madam's Organ. Guys like Chinna used to hang around and go up to the house where they were practicing. Chinna will talk to you for hours about the spirits and reggae and how to eat and what to do. Smoke weed and play music all day—that was his philosophy. And I guess H.R. picked up on it. His book changed from *Think and Grow Rich* to the Bible. He started carrying the Bible around.

EARL HUDSON

We always went to church as kids, so we always knew who the true and living God is: Jesus. And through meeting certain bredrens and being conscious of certain things, and knowing where certain history lies, we came into knowing about Rasta.

JULIAN CAMBRIDGE | FRIEND, MUSICIAN

I witnessed him with the PMA book, then a Bible and his diet. I watched him go from the mohawk to PMA to Rasta to whatever he's doing now. I was one of the first people he met that was involved in Rasta business. To be a true Rastaman, you have to believe that Haile Selassie is God. H.R. went on and did his thing. I didn't introduce him to the faith and all that. It started like a snowball, and he took it from there. It was for him to accept it or not. We started off by being musicians and eating food and smoking weed, and we knew all these other musicians who were Rastas back then. It just went from there to here—what we have now.

---

[6]*I and I: a Rasfafarian term that refers to the oneness of Jah and all people*

RUSSELL BRAEN

The Bible became very important to H.R. He was struggling to touch base with history, and with being a black man in a basically white scene. Some of the Rastafarians in Adams Morgan at the time, Chinna and some of the others, helped H.R. find that there was some space there for him to be spiritual in. He wanted to have more meaning than just the music business. He was really struggling to come up with something. Even PMA, I don't think, was doing enough for him at that point.

MARK ANDERSEN

Essentially, H.R. goes toward this particular expression of the Bible. It's not just mainstream Christianity as we know it. He goes to Rasta, which is not only connected deeply to reggae music but to the specific black power liberation theology. It is a radical stand on behalf of the dispossessed. It's challenging the system. It's fire on Babylon. You want the system to fall. It fits perfectly in a way with punk rock. Looking back, it was tailor-made to be the salvation for H.R., and he takes to it—like he has taken to everything else—with this incredible fervor. It was something that would change his life for good. In the short term, it helps him kick heroin, but it also turns the band in a direction that, I think it's fair to say, would undermine if not destroy their immediate commercial potential. But it took them to a deeper, higher and more powerful place. Joseph turned his life over to Rastafari. He grabbed onto it like a life preserver in a stormy sea. On top of the PMA stuff, he brought in the Rastafarian aspect, which brought an even harder-edged, more radical edge to the politics. This sense of the apocalypse coming, and imminent revolution, was essential to taking that last little step to making the Bad Brains that band which was just unparalleled.

QUESTLOVE

I never associated Bad Brains with things you normally associated with punk or fast music. Just the fact that they introduced Rastafari and dub and true roots reggae to that genre is absolutely unreal. I now understand why so many fans are into both genres. It led them to investigate and discover music they had never known before. I have always seen it as "spiritual rabble-rousing." I know there's anger, but there can be a strong spiritual association. It's passion. I mean, you see that in some black Baptist churches; you see that same passion. Music is probably the most pure, spiritual execution that a human being can use to communicate.

IAN MACKAYE

DC already had a pretty thriving underground scene. The Razz were a very important band, The Slickee Boys were important, The Penetrators were very important, and there was Snitch, who ended up becoming Black Market Baby. There were a lot of these arty, new wave rock bands, too, like Urban Verbs, and Tony Perkins and the Psychotics. But Bad Brains were coming out of somewhere totally different. You would hear these reports about these guys walking around Georgetown handing out fliers. *Bad Brains: are they a band or what?* I think maybe they had done one show at that point. I believe it was June of '79, and I went to the Bayou, which was a rock club down on K Street in Georgetown, to see The Damned. It was the first time they had been to Washington, DC. I was seventeen and had to use a fake ID to bullshit my way into the club. Bad Brains were opening for The Damned, and we were, like, "Wow, these are the guys we've been seeing around," and they were phenomenal! We were just like, "Whoa, all right. These guys are from *here.*" We had seen bands like The Slickee Boys, and we'd seen other local bands, but Bad Brains just

took it to another level. We were so blown away by them. The Damned liked them so much they invited them to come tour England with them. This was the original incarnation of punk, so H.R. was a very Johnny Rotten kind of guy. At that point, we had seen pictures of punks and we had heard the records, but we had no idea how they moved. There was no video or film. Obviously, no computers—nothing to look at. You just hadn't seen anything, so actually seeing people move was pretty phenomenal. H.R.'s charisma was undeniable onstage. It was just mind-blowing, and he was just so animated in terms of running back and forth across the stage. I'm not sure if he jumped off the balcony that night, but I know I saw him at The Bayou other times when he jumped off the balcony. Gary was in his full Dr. Know regalia. He had full scrubs on with blood all over them. Darryl was still called Darryl Cyanide, and he had bleached blonde hair. Just their presence—they weren't asking for nothing. They were just telling us what was up. As a kid, you see the arena rock world where opening bands are usually the subject of people booing them off the stage like, "Bring on Van Halen" or whoever the headliner is. Openers are largely treated like the small acts before the main ones, and with the early punk shows, you still kind of had that. So with The Damned opening slot, most bands would have been chewed up, like a feeding frenzy for the audience. Bad Brains: this was just not the case. They had a spot, and they were going to do it. They were obviously working hard. That really sent a message to us like, that's a band that's from here and they're better than any band we've seen up to that point.

ALEC MACKAYE

Their sound had a lot of rock 'n' roll in there. I remember them playing Black Sabbath's "Paranoid," and several amazing covers that just came out of nowhere, that were not what you would expect necessarily. Because punk rock was about turning away from all of that, but they were incorporating this rock 'n' roll sound, and the speed was what was adding so much; there was this brutal sound. They were loud, and they were accurate and they were just unbelievably fast, and H.R.'s singing in particular, was all that everybody could talk about.

JOHN STABB | GOVERNMENT ISSUE

H.R. had almost like a Screamin' Jay Hawkins thing mixed with punk rock. Just a phenomenal, incredibly powerful force onstage, and he was a huge influence on a lot of people. He definitely influenced the hell out of Henry Rollins and Minor Threat and all that stuff. For G.I., when I first put out *Legless Bull,* my goal at the time was to put out a record that's faster than the Bad Brains. Yeah, it may have been faster, but that doesn't mean it was better. H.R. jumping and doing all this stuff with intensity, and the stops and starts and tightness of the band, it can never be replaced. They were like God's gift to DC at the time.

MICHAEL FRANTI

His vocal stylings were very unique. He was like a jazz saxophonist, taking things from really high to down low, all over the place, and sometimes atonal to the music. It didn't have to be perfect pitch all the time. It was always about this energy and this veracity of getting the message out.

H.R.

We wanted to have an original sound. Earl, Darryl, Gary and I wanted to do something that no other group had thought about doing. These brothers were slapping out these rhythms, and it touched me in such a way that I knew we were ready to deliver our message, which was love, hard work and the best music in creation.

ALEC MACKAYE

They didn't do things quite the way a lot of other bands might do things, which would be to try to incorporate themselves into the existing DC scene. Bad Brains seemed to just arrive. Not arrived like, "Hello. We're here," but they came in like gangbusters, blazing into it. They were never apologetic, more like take no prisoners—all the time really full tilt. Which was kind of frustrating for some bands that want to have more of a community, I guess. They really had their own approach and just set themselves apart. They didn't wait around for people to help them out and do things. They were like, "Who's got what we need? We'll go there."

IAN MACKAYE

There were all these issues in rock music at the time, and in England there was this racist stuff that the National Front kind of got involved with. Some pretty well-known musicians had taken a position which was consistent with the National Front. So there was a Rock Against Racism show in England with The Clash and a bunch of bands, and the idea was to show that musicians would rock against racism. H.R. was really interested in that. I think he also took note that ninety-five percent of the people at the Rock Against Racism show were white because it was punk rock. He got this idea to do shows in a project in DC called Valley Green. He had some kind of connection there, and H.R. said, "We're gonna do our own Rock Against Racism shows, but we're just gonna go play to black people."

LUCIAN PERKINS | PHOTOJOURNALIST

We had President Carter at the time, we had the Iranian hostage situation, and you had Ronald Reagan ready to be ushered in. You had a city in Washington, DC, that was extremely divided between the whites and the blacks. You had Marion Barry as the mayor. DC at that time was very divisive and a lot of people never ventured outside their own neighborhoods. Going to Valley Green was almost like walking into a different country, going from Northwest Washington to Southeast Washington. It was one of the poorer areas in the country, much less Washington, DC.

IAN MACKAYE

It was the Bad Brains and Trenchmouth in 1979. And then in 1980, we did it again, but this time it was the Bad Brains, Teen Idles and The Untouchables. It was a courtyard and they just ran an extension cord out of an apartment window for power. It was all the kids in the neighborhood, and these little kids were just going crazy in the front, and the older kids kinda grittin' in the back. It was a pretty crazy experience. His idea was to just take the music to the people. Those kids found us ridiculous. We looked funny. We were punk rockers, and our music was probably indecipherable to them—just fast and crazy.

ALEC MACKAYE

The Untouchables are playing, and there's this kid next to me. As soon as the first song is done, the kid was like, "Hey, you finished?" And I was like, "Uh, no, we've got more songs," and he was like, "Oh, okay." Then after the second song, he was like, "You guys finished yet?" I say, "No, man, we've got like fifteen songs," or whatever. Finally, we're done and I was like, "We're done," and he goes, "Okay, can I play my radio over the microphone?" He just came up, got his boombox next to the microphone, pressed play on the radio and everybody went bananas! Until then, people were just standing there watching us. I remember people standing about five feet away from me, and the little kids coming up and touching my bleached hair. For the Bad Brains, there was never a question about this being the wrong kind of venue or anything like that. They were just comfortable doing the thing they were doing, wherever they were doing it. What H.R. had in mind with Rock Against Racism was the simplest thing: There's a racial divide, let's close it. I grew up in DC and always loved my city, and this was a moment of like, there's a little gap here and it helped close that gap. It wasn't ten thousand people, it was just a handful of people, but it made a difference. His idea was achieved.

LUCIAN PERKINS

It was a scene of contrast. You had poor inner-city folks, with a group of white suburban kids dressed up as punk rockers. You couldn't have dreamed of anything more surreal in a scene. On some level, each side was very curious

about the other, and it was interesting watching people try to size each other up and try to figure out what was going on. And the kids from Valley Green did not like the music at all. It was so alien to what they listened to. Most of them didn't know what to make of it. But on a certain level, I think everybody had a good time. It was a clash of cultures, but I think everybody came away with something. A lot of them had never seen a white person—literally—and I think it shook up a lot of stereotypes.

ALEC MACKAYE

H.R. was interested in what we were doing and not just a little bit. He wanted to know what people were up to. He was really into conversation in a way that I didn't expect. I thought he was incredibly cool, and he didn't have to talk to me or anything. My brother had an old Duster with a tape deck, but he didn't have speakers in the back, so we had regular speakers that we wired up. You had to hold them on your lap. I was sitting in the back seat with H.R. and we're listening to the Bad Brains tape, and it's just blowing our minds. When it's done, H.R. turns to me and goes, "What about you guys? Do you have the tape yet? Let's listen to yours." He was very inclusive and interested in what everybody was doing at work, and he leaned towards things that were complex. I feel like that's why Madam's Organ got pulled into all this. Part of why they had music there was because they needed rent money, and part of why people played there was because there were no rules. But H.R. had an affinity towards the people there, and was interested in all of their crazy ideas. That's a curious mind; someone who wants to know about the world.

IAN MACKAYE

That was a pretty incredible time. For me, the Bad Brains around 1980 were the greatest band in the world, and in many ways, are still the greatest band in the world to me.

They were just that good. And H.R. was such a visionary kind of guy. He was always about, "Let's do it. We can do it. Let's do this." Everything was always, "We can do this." I don't know if I would ever call H.R. a hardcore punk. I would say the music was pretty inspirational for people. It played a role in terms of the precision and speed and impact of it. If you listen to Minor Threat, it is a different form. We were definitely inspired by them, clearly. We saw them play and we were like, "Wow, let's do that." So I think that they were heavily inspirational to us, but we were never peers. In a way, it's like they were elders for us. S.O.A. and Minor Threat and Government Issue and Youth Brigade and all those bands; we sort of saw ourselves as peers. I think the Bad Brains were in a slightly different place. They were from a different world. They were a little older and they had different motivations.

5. BANNED IN DC 1979–1981

DC was pretty cool. It was the Reagan years and there was always news about the President and things going on in the White House. The threat of World War III was constant, too. Really, we just heard that there were a lot more places to play in New York.

-H.R.

IAN MACKAYE

The guys often talk about there having been nowhere to play in DC. That might be the case if you want to be a working musician and you want to make a living from your music. You've got to go to New York or LA. In DC, it's almost impossible to make a living by playing gigs. So part of world domination is you finish with your town, and you go to the next one. I remember very clearly seeing them at The Childe Harold, which was a club in Dupont Circle, and I remember being outside after the show hanging out. Mo had bought the band a van and Earl was sitting in the driver's seat, and

I said, "What are you guys up to?" And they said, "Oh, we're moving to New York." I was shocked! "You're moving to New York? You're gonna leave Washington?! How can you leave Washington?!" I just think that was their next move, and that's what they did. They were just trying to be ambitious.

EARL HUDSON

When we opened for The Damned at The Bayou, they loved us. After that, we'd gone up to New York to play a show, I believe at CBGB, and they had a show up there, too, so we went to see them play. We were hanging out with Dave Vanian and them, and they said they wanted to produce us, so we were like, "Hell yeah!"

They wanted to bring us over to England, so our next move as Bad Brains was to go and conquer New York. We go up to New York primarily to fly out of there to go over to England. To help get the money for the plane tickets, I sold my drums, and we met some friends up in New York who were going to help us with additional money. We got the money up and we had a friend of ours who was kind of managing us. He happened to have this little vial, but it didn't have anything in there. Maybe it was from before we flew over to England, but anyway, we made it over to England and we're at the airport going through customs. The customs people found this little vial, which had probably been used for some cocaine or whatever, and they said, "No, you guys are not coming in here." The cats from The Damned were there trying to get us in, but customs took our passports from us and put us back on a plane to New York. We had two customized guitars that were somehow stolen between us arriving and going back, plus I had sold my drums, so we're back on a plane, with no passports and no gear. We didn't get our passports back until we landed back in New York.

That's how that went. We were living in New York after we got back, and we didn't have any money. Living off of shows and a bag of chips a day and whatever. A couple of times eating at the Salvation Army until a show came up. It wasn't easy, man. We stayed in New York for a while and just kicked it using equipment from this other band, The Stimulators, who were friends of ours.

MARK ANDERSEN

So, they are in New York City having just been booted from England, and they are literally having their Christmas meal in a soup kitchen line. Back in DC, there's this word-of-mouth building after The Damned show. But we're in this place with a lot of these shiny white monuments built by slaves. This is a city that in my lifetime was profoundly segregated. Let's just say there was an extra edge from some of the white folks towards this extraordinary African-American punk band. I mean, punks themselves were scary, but then the racial factor and Rasta is really scaring people, so it was very difficult for the band to find places to play. They were never officially "Banned in DC," as the song goes, but it was something close to that.

JOHN JOSEPH

H.R. in them days didn't even really have dreads. When I met them they were so punk rock, but they were just starting to get into Rasta. In New York, everybody talks about punk rock and New York Hardcore or whatever. When the Bad Brains came to New York they created this whole thing you see today. It was all created by the Bad Brains. I watched them go from playing shows with fifty people not giving a fuck who the Bad Brains were, to playing to thousands—and it happened quick. I even saw them play with The Clash at Bonds—and even The Clash were like, "How the fuck do we go on after that?!"

H.R.

We wound up getting a break in New York from a dude named Jimmi Quidd who played in The Dots. We met Jimmi, and he said he knew of a recording studio, so we recorded our "Pay to Cum" single. Up until that point, people had asked me if I wanted to put out records, and I said, "No, the band is not ready yet," but I knew Darryl, Earl and Gary had it in them. I just wanted us to be the best of all time, the best band that was ever created.

PAY TO CUM b/w STAY CLOSE TO ME

AD BRAINS ARE:

H.R. .... LEAD VOCALS
EARL HUDSON .... DRUMS
DARRYL JENIFER .... BASS GUITAR
DR. KNOW .... GUITARS

CED: JIMMI QUIDD "A PRANK PRODUCTION"
)ED: DOTS STUDIO, NEW YORK, N.Y.
ERS: STEVE HORTON and REESE VIRGIN
ND REMIXED: STEVE HORTON and REESE VIRGIN
ED: DECEMBER 1979
RAPHY: CHARLES DAVIS and PAUL BISHOW
S: MAB INC.
D: BOB LUDWIG AT MASTERDISK CORP, N.Y., N.Y.
ION: "ASSISTANCE" LEIGH SIORIS

SPECIAL THANKS TO:

THE MAD, THE DOTS, THE STIMULATORS,
STEVE HORTON, JIMMI QUIDD, JOHN BOUZAKIS,
ILIES AND EVERYONE WHO MADE THIS ALL POSSIBLE

i FAN CLUB:
REPLY, SEND SELF ADDRESSED ENVELOPE TO:
BAD BRAINS
1821 BRIERSFIELD ROAD
OXON HILL, MARYLAND 20021

© 1979 BAD BRAINS

Pay to Cum!

Bad Brains

ALEC MACKAYE

Everybody got excited when somebody they knew made a record, and that's how it was when Bad Brains recorded "Pay to Cum." H.R. gave me a copy, and I was so excited. I took it home and was surprised that the production quality was so clean. I also thought that Earl had done some kind of trick. I couldn't believe he could drum that fast. It just seemed impossible, and I remember drilling him like, "Come on, for real. You did not play this fast." He's just one of these guys that made it seem effortless. We called him Cool Earl.

He never even broke a sweat, it seemed. I'm sure he was working hard back there, but he just looked undisturbed. I know nowadays people can do those kinds of things, but it was the fastest thing I had heard.

It became like a pastime for us to try and sing the lyrics at the same speed as H.R. I could never do it, but Henry Rollins came pretty close. He would jump up onstage and sing the whole song with them. They were untouchable in that way with their speed.

EARL HUDSON

I came up with some tax refund money and put it towards getting that record made. We recorded it in New York and came back down to DC and pressed it up and got the cover made. H.R. and Gary would sit down and fold each one, and the rest of the band would take one single out at a time and place the vinyl inside. There were a limited number of copies. We only had about five hundred. We were selling those at shows and carrying on. That's around the time when H.R. found Mo Sussman.

H.R.

Mo Sussman worked at a restaurant in Washington, DC, and we went to see him one day because a friend at Madam's Organ told us there was a man who might be available for management. He took us into his office, and we let him know that we wanted him to be our manager. He was an honest person, but he didn't exactly want to make our ideals a priority.

ALEC MACKAYE

I knew who Mo was, but I will never understand entirely how they ever got together with him. That was a totally bizarre episode in their careers as far as I'm concerned.

MO SUSSMAN | EARLY BAD BRAINS MANAGER

The Bad Brains popped up at Max's Kansas City in New York, and I remembered that just earlier the *Washington Post* had done a story about the punk movement in DC, which featured them, so I wanted to meet the group. H.R. comes bounding into the restaurant and jumps into a chair across the bar, and I physically was forced back. I know that sounds like bullshit, but I physically was repelled by this aura that was around him to the point where I just had to settle myself down. *What was that?!* That's a true story. I know people find it hard to believe, but my first introduction to H.R. was feeling his aura—feeling his power.

I knew right then and there that I had to do something with these guys, 'cause someone who has that power, there is something mystical involved in that. I had developed some music business contacts with CBS Records and EMI. In fact, my daughter Jennifer became very close to the president of EMI Records in London, who had helped with The Beatles. So I had the contacts to get the Bad Brains a record deal, but they didn't believe they were quite ready yet. In my opinion they had it, but they weren't ready. I did get them a gig at the 9:30 Club and showcased them for CBS Records, Warner Brothers and EMI. I had three or four record people there and I introduced the Bad Brains. I was quoted as saying, "They are going to be the black Beatles."

MARK ANDERSEN

Ironically, as they're embracing this radical black-power, apocalyptic Christian faith, Mo Sussman says to them, "Hey, I wanna make you superstars!" And so this suit-and-tie guy offers them a lot of money to, you know, make it happen. They get some new equipment; he gets them a place to practice. There's a farm out in Herndon that he basically turned over to them as their place to live, because they're essentially homeless. But Mo says, "You gotta clean up your image. You gotta play the game!" Well, Joseph's not very good at playing the game. It's one of his great gifts—one of the things that is really inspirational about him. And it's also, I'm sure, one of the things that made him so aggravating to the rest of the band. Because if there's one thing you could count on, and I'm not saying this lightly: if you get a good deal going, Joseph's going to fuck it up. Mo must have sunk $20,000 or more into the band, but the band is turning into Rastafarian outlaws in front of his eyes.

H.R.

He wanted me to wear spandex and Jockey tank top shirts, and I didn't want to go on the stage with a leotard on. I didn't want to fall for some fashion syndrome. I didn't want that reaction. I thought those people wanted to hear good music, so we just delivered that good music.

MO SUSSMAN

I went, "Holy mackerel, this is really something," but the record people didn't get it. So after that, I held back on trying to make a contract work, but I knew we had something. We were going to be at CBGB, and we were staying at the Plaza Hotel. We're having lunch on an outside patio across from the hotel, and this cute young girl was the waitress. She asks, "What do you guys do?" "Well, that's the band," I said, "the Bad Brains." She said, "Oh, the Bad Brains. I'm going to see them tonight!" This cute, perky gal was actually going to see this band. There were some moments that reinforced that I was right on track.

MARK ANDERSEN

Basically, they're undergoing this transformation that brings them full bore into this extraordinary mating of PMA, punk rock and Rastafarianism. It immediately changes the way they look, and it adds even more of a radical and incredible

focus to what they're doing. It also, of course, led to trouble
with Mo Sussman. Joseph and Mo had long discussions
about how music is for the people. Joseph telling him, "You
know, it should be free—like a gift from God." And Mo is like,
"Yeah but, you know, somebody's gotta pay for your food,
and somebody's gotta pay for your rent, and for musical
instruments." And it just came to a head. Clearly, Joseph
was not going to take the direction that Mo needed him to in
order to make it big. Mo thought they could be big if they'd
just listen to him. That's when the Mo stuff falls apart.

EARL HUDSON

I guess in the end, we were just too rebellious or something for Mo. We were still going through certain phases, and things like new wave came along, which gave us a new type of dressing. That's where wearing suits and ties for a bit came from, but we kind of dashed that aside and kept on doing what we were doing. Mo just wanted us to go commercial and make some money already.

JOHN JOSEPH

Around that time, the late '70s, New York City was fucking ready to explode. The city was broke, there had been the Son of Sam, there was the punk rock summer, the garbage strike, police corruption, the fucking blackout. But at the same time, with all the insanity that was going on, you had on a parallel track the most amazing art—and I mean art in a sense of punk rock—and all of this amazing stuff coming out of this city. That shit just kept going through all the muck, and punk rock managed to keep swimming in that river of shit that was NYC in the late '70s. We were in the thick of the shit here, and I think that's why when the Bad Brains came here, they just put a stamp on it like, "This is what it's about, and this is the reaction we need to have to what we are experiencing." They were here at that time, and they lived it.

JACK RABID | THE BIG TAKEOVER

The punk rock scene in New York, around '78/'79 was in flux. The original 1973 to 1977 CBGB and Max's bands had either broken up or graduated to playing theaters. Now you were seeing the Talking Heads at the Beacon Theatre, and Television was playing the Palladium. Patti Smith wasn't playing anymore for the most part. This was a second wave of the club scene, and much like the original one, it started in small places. It centered around The Stimulators, The

Mad, The Dots, The Blessed, and The Heartbreakers. That was fun, that little club scene with forty or fifty people attending every week. Anytime I knew those bands were playing, or the Misfits came in from New Jersey for one of their extremely rare shows—and to throw the Bad Brains into the mix was fantastic. The more they played, the more the legend of the Bad Brains spread.

JIMMY GESTAPO

There was an incredible music scene here in New York then. We were out all the time, and there were shows all the time. In one night you could go to three or four different clubs to see bands. I had been introduced to this music by The Stimulators and the Dead Kennedys, and S.O.A. and Minor Threat, and I heard about these black guys, these amazing black guys. I literally was told about them while I was on my way to go see them. Sure enough, they were a bunch of amazing black guys playing amazing punk rock. They changed the whole New York scene, and it changed the game for everybody.

JACK RABID

When they first came to New York, they were much slower in terms of tempo than where they ended up, but the songs were already incredibly fast by the standards of that time. They were basically jazz cats who landed on the planet and turned into the hardest, most extreme punk rock band you could think of. They made the Sex Pistols look like Menudo or something—although I loved the Sex Pistols. The only reason I knew about them was because a couple of other punk rockers told me, "Don't argue with me. The next time you see their name in the *Village Voice*, just go to wherever it is they're playing. Cancel anything else you were gonna do that night."

JOHN JOSEPH

After seeing H.R. that first time, he could have had me worshiping cocoa puffs. I would have done it. There's a saying: "Whatever action a great man performs, common men follow." His example, and the message behind the lyrics when you started opening them songs up—revolution, spiritual revolution, consciousness, positive mental attitude—was like some mystic punk and harder than all the rest. Nobody could fuckin' touch him.

H.R.

In the early days we did not have our own equipment. We would just cruise around to different locations, and we would ask people if we could use their equipment, and I would sing my songs about PMA. When kids in the audience heard our group, they would kind of go *snap, crackle, pop,* and pandemonium would spread. I'm going up there and dancing all crazy, doing flips and cartwheels and diving off the stage into the audience. The backflips came from Jamaica. When I was two and three years old, I would stand on my bed, bounce up and down, and flip over. I went to the beach, and while I was under water, I was practicing flips and standing on my hands, and that's how it started. Later I became a gymnast and a swimmer in school, and teachers would train us to do certain dives and one-and-a-halves and that kind of thing.

IAN MACKAYE

Bob Marley and other reggae guys would talk about, "mash it up." It was a reggae kind of saying. This is a ridiculous theory of mine, but I think H.R. probably said "mash it up," but because of his accent, which had this Rasta inflection, the New York kids heard, "MOSH it up," and their dancing became "moshing." It's just a theory, but I haven't heard a better one. I know he would say, "mash it up," so "MOSH it up." I think that's where the term "moshing" originated. I could be wrong.

H.R.

We didn't know that "mashing it up" meant start tearing the club up. That's what they thought we were saying. We weren't saying that at all. I was just using the term to express exuberance and jubilance. Anyway, one day I was dancing and I dove out and everybody moved, and I landed flat on my face on the floor. Nobody was there to catch me.

EARL HUDSON

It wasn't rehearsed. That was just him. We said we were gonna be the hardest and the fastest, so you know, that was his athletic background coming out. You have to put it all out there. With everything you do in music, it's coming from your soul and your heart, and you can't be up there lollygagging and shit. We set this precedent.

ANTHONY COUNTEY

When H.R. started singing, I just couldn't believe it. He was so fucking good! It's like the band expressed an absolute confidence in something extremely positive in the middle of a very dark thunderous occurrence. That was really stunning. And H.R. danced. The way he took Doc, Darryl and Earl's music with his lyrics, and how he moved became the way the whole New York scene fucking moved. It was *his* enthusiasm that got us all enthusiastic. And there were some other great bands around. The Stimulators were a great band, but with the Bad Brains, it was just so locked down. It was so absolutely uncontrived and intense, and that uncontrived intensity became the whole scene. It was just different from everybody else. It had the same emotional references as some of the great, bigger rock bands—the Grateful Dead, the Stones—but somehow, it was fresh. They were black and their music was pure, and it wasn't like anything you'd heard or seen before.

MICHAEL FRANTI

I think what made H.R. so compelling was the mix of incredible anger and incredible love going on at the same time. You didn't see many black people playing loud guitars at that time. You didn't see black people on stage talking about militant social issues. You didn't see a lot of black people with dreadlocks at that time. And to combine all those things—being louder, faster, angrier and having a cooler hairstyle than any other punk rock bands that were out there—was so unique and so strong. The only other thing I can compare it to, and it was years later, was the first time I saw Public Enemy. Feeling that same way . . . like this is so powerful and so strong and so together. The music is so unique, the voice is so angry, the performance is so tough that it scares people.

JIMMY GESTAPO

I'm pretty sure it was at a Stimulators show that they opened. It was one of my first shows, first time on the dance floor. It wasn't like it is now; it used to be just skanking in place, and it was the greatest thing. Someone picked up all the tables in Max's, threw them into a pile and everybody started dancing. To see H.R. with the energy that he had, doing backflips and stuff in such a small space, never mind to be doing it at as the lead singer. I was used to seeing KISS, a bunch of poseurs. The music was so powerful, it drove you to do that and drove you to want to jump into stuff and run around. CBGB had theater seats bolted to the floor in front of the stage then, and I remember Harley Flanagan and I kicking the theater seats out. There was not that much space between the stage and the front row of the theater seats, so we just smashed them out. I don't think they ever put them back in after that.

JOHN JOSEPH

New York then was pogoing to bands, looking like it was a fucking epileptic seizure. And H.R., if you watch the way that he moved onstage, he did that skank, just throwing himself, fucking rocking it. Plus, that whole creepy-crawling shit H.R. used to do onstage during the intro to "Big Take Over," it was like this tribal dance and H.R. was the tribe leader. It was just this energy between the audience and the band.

AL ANDERSON | THE WAILERS, H.R. BAND

I used to see him at the Mudd Club and CBGB and got to know him really well. We would smoke herb and talk about what it was like working with Bob, Peter and Bunny and being in Jamaica, because he's part Jamaican. I thought

his lyrical level was really high. It's important to know that even this type of "ooh baby" shit he's talking about was about what's inside the heart and the struggles normal people have to go through day by day.

MICHAEL FRANTI

The message that came across to a young person like me, was that there are a lot of things happening in the world where human beings are put second to corporations' needs, or the needs of governments, or whoever is rich and in power. His message was about the empowerment of people, especially people that are oppressed. That really resonated with me because I was adopted, and I grew up in a family where I didn't feel like I fit in. I felt: here's somebody else in the world that felt the same way I did, that people left out should still have a voice.

JIMMY GESTAPO

Once you get over hearing just the chaos of him singing and the energy, then you find out that there is also a message in it. When you're a kid and you're into punk, it's like punks get fucked up and have fun. Then all of a sudden, you start to find out the political consciousness in the message of punk and hardcore. It doesn't come across with some bands, but with them, there was a big message, and it definitely opened my head up to a lot of things.

JOHN JOSEPH

Look at the lyrics to those songs. It's prophecy, man. "FVK," "Big Take Over," "I," all of these fucking songs. Never has there been a greater need for that message than right now. Everybody just hears a record, but H.R. lived every word on that fucking record. I got to see that first hand. To this day, people hear that album and just start an investigative journey. Musicians are trying to figure out what Doc and

Earl are playing, and then if you have any kind of inclination toward spirituality, or consciousness, or culture, or even politics, then you are going to listen to H.R.'s words and investigate. H.R.'s message can smash the conditioning and the dumbing down that's going on. The person who wrote these lyrics—that's the real motherfucker you all need to be investigating.

H.R.

We met Jerry Williams and he had a little rehearsal and recording studio called 171 A. It was right near Tompkins Square Park, not too far from A7, a club we performed at. A lot of punk rock and hardcore kids would go there and they would have after-parties. That's where the group started recording for Neil Cooper and Reachout International Records. We met Neil at CBGB. He said he was going to put out these cool cassettes and he could give us not a whole lot, but just something that would make an album worthwhile. And we said, "Yes." The rest is just a miracle of God, because we got our first album out.

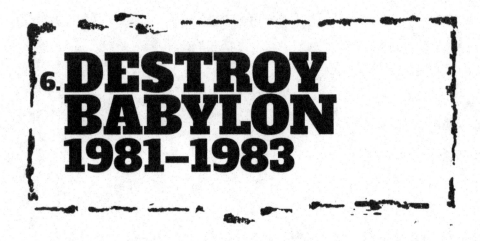

6. DESTROY BABYLON 1981–1983

We wanted to teach I and I to love I and I. Teach people to love Jah and stay away from negativity as tempting as it is.

-H.R.

JOHN JOSEPH

As my friend the late, great Adam Yauch said: "The Bad Brains ROIR cassette is the greatest punk/hardcore album of all time." And hands down, it is. I was there for every minute of that recording with Jay Dublee, God rest his soul. I will never forget that. When that shit hit the streets . . . you know when you see those maps with something spreading all over the country? That's what happened. It was like the litmus test for the rest of the fucking planet.

ANGELO MOORE

My first cassette was that Bad Brains ROIR tape. I was listening to it and I thought they were some white boys playing punk rock. Then I saw the picture and was like, "Wow! They're black just like me." I'll put it to you like this: the Bad Brains were the first band that made me feel like it was okay to be black and play punk rock and be just like all the punkers I'd seen on the street. They broke a whole stereotype right there, so it made me think it's all right to have a fuckin' mohawk and a chain and be punk. Before that, I thought it was only for white people. They were really liberating.

JIMMY GESTAPO

I was there with them when they recorded it. It still spanks anything else that is out now recorded by all you fancy-pants Pro Tools fruits. Amazing four-track, real analog. All these people's fancy gadgets and computers, and they still can't replicate the purity and the energy of that recording. You get simplicity in tubes. You get it warts and all.

MARK ANDERSEN

That recording was an incredible representation of the band, but the band was in a difficult position because, on one hand, they were a revolutionary band. Anybody who saw them knew that. I remember a guy from Sick of It All talking about how going to see the Bad Brains wasn't just some show, it was a revolution! You were being called upon to rise up and rebel. Not just metaphorically, real revolution. That is a testament to the power of the band and their commitment. On the other hand, they're living down in Alphabet City, and it was hard.

H.R.

A young man gave us a place to stay. He had rooms available in a building down between Avenue C and D, but there were no windows in the building, so we had to put up plastic with tape. That's what pulled us through, but we did stay at George from The Mad's house. Mad George was a bit bizarre. He had a lot of silly, goofy toys, and he would go through his stuff,

and all of a sudden, he would have like a fake hand, or a fake piece of brain, or somebody's chest with their head missing. We stayed there for about a year. Although it was cold in the wintertime, in the summertime and springtime it was very good and we'd go see different bands perform, and the Brains would play at a place called A7. 171 A was close by. You could meet people who were artists, and drama students, and that for me was inspiring. Then, of course, we met some of the brothers from the 12 Tribes of Israel and eventually found the 12 Tribes headquarters. We got to reason with some of the bredrens about the Bible and the Scriptures, Armageddon, holocaust. Eventually, a new movement took place, and we changed our eating habits and we changed our thinking habits. For instance, we stayed away from pork and bacon and instead ate more tofu and fruit and rice. Another thing was we stayed away from was hard drugs, and we got away from alcohol. Instead, we would sip tea and drink Ital juices and roots and spring water.

ANTHONY COUNTEY

I was at Roseland and Bad Brains were opening for Gang of Four. I knew the promoters for the show, so they got me in the back room. The dressing room was absolutely packed with people, and it seemed like there was nobody in charge of anything. The promoters came back and were like, "Okay, you are on in fifteen minutes." I had just spoken to Darryl for the first time, and he had just gone to go get pizza because he was hungry. So I saw Frank the promoter, and I told him that they were not coming out in fifteen minutes, because the bass player had just gone out but would be back in fifteen minutes, so we will try to get them onstage after that. They were like, "Okay, Anthony, cool." So Darryl came back, and they went onstage. I wasn't necessarily looking to manage any bands, but they needed and wanted somebody to help them. They wanted somebody to really do the management thing, so that's what I did. It was really instant what they did, which was just show up at my house sometime after that show. My friend who got me on the guest list told them where I lived on East 9th Street. There was a job to be done. I had to get them on the road, get them recorded, introduce them to the right people.

SAUL WILLIAMS | MUSICIAN, ACTOR, WRITER, POET

I think it's important for an artist to choose their own path. I think it's important for an artist to decide which route they want to take. When you're bringing things that are original to the table, it's hard to take advice from someone who's sitting behind a desk trying to get you to fit into some sort of thing that already exists when you know they're not clever enough to realize that you are the example.

ANTHONY COUNTEY

It wasn't easy from the beginning, but I'd be, like, "Okay," and let them have it how they wanted it. In the music industry, a lot of times, management or whatever will have an idea like, *Oh, this is how you should sound, or you should try this, or do a cover of that song.* They really had a very clear idea. They at least believed that they knew what they were doing. They didn't want any influence from anybody else, so that was a positive thing for me because I was not looking to contrive anything. I'm not very different from their attitude, so the idea of marketing never came into it. Sure, I tried to get labels and the people I knew in the music industry to know that the band was there. And bringing like a thousand kids in places like New York and LA, and in other places. If people knew about them, they came. They were too hot to handle, really.

At the time, they were basically squatting. It was rough. The money came at a show or whatever, but then quickly, the money was gone. The band had to play and had to do things to stay alive, so around the time they did the ROIR tape, we went on tour. That's what you have to do. You have to go on tour. I

found support, and we went across America. There was no way that people could know about them being there in most towns. They would have to have known somebody from LA or New York or DC who told them to go see this fucking band. But that was the line: "You have to see this fucking band."

DUFF MCKAGAN | GUNS N' ROSES

I saw them in 1981 or '82 at a place called Under the Rail in Seattle. I was really into that song "Pay to Cum" and had that single on vinyl. I also had a single by a band called The Upstarts, and both bands were touring together. I didn't really know what to expect from seeing the Bad Brains. I just had the vinyl to go on. We had fanzines, and that's how we found out what was going on with bands like Black Flag and DOA and Minor Threat and so forth. The Upstarts came all the way from England, which was very exotic for us Seattle kids back in the day. So the Bad Brains and Upstarts play together. Bad Brains came on and totally blew all forty of our minds at that little club.

JOHN JOSEPH

I did that first tour with them and was always like, "Wait until these motherfuckers see this shit. They are going to flip." And they did. Sometimes heads flipped the wrong way. When they would play down South, all these club owners, these bikers and shit who run these clubs, didn't know they were a black band. And they'd be saying shit like "Get these niggers out of my club," pulling the plug on them, you know—crazy shit.

MARK ANDERSEN

Up until that point, we've seen Joseph largely as this extraordinary stage figure. The band is getting out and playing for more people than ever, the ROIR cassette is spreading their fame, and the word-of-mouth around them is ferocious and overwhelmingly positive. People like Jello Biafra from Dead Kennedys are worshipping at the altar, as a lot of folks did, because they were just that good. However, they are on the road, and let's just say that before they left Greenwich Village, they have some encounter with kind of this emerging, assertive gay milieu.

They are there with their religious fervor, and the Bad Brains thought they were living between Sodom and Gomorrah back in New York. The next day, they're on their way to LA, where they do an interview with *Flipside* magazine and this is where the third Joseph appears. For the first time, at least in such a broad public context, he says reprehensible things about gay people. Now, this is the band of revolution, peace, love and unity, so people couldn't quite get their heads around this. MDC, who were playing a show with them, had bisexual members and sometimes cross-dressed. They were flipping out when they heard this, because again, it's like they're bowing down at the altar of Bad Brains, and then this comes out.

Bad Brains would move on to Texas, which is where MDC is from, and there's this terrible incident that happens with members of the Big Boys. They played a show with the Big Boys in Austin, and by all accounts it was an incredible show. Somehow or another, it becomes obvious that Biscuit, the lead singer of Big Boys is gay, and Joseph just totally freaks out and called him a "bloodclot faggot." There were claims that Biscuit made a pass at H.R., but what probably happened was Biscuit gave him a hug and said he was great or whatever. Why does that cause anybody to flip out? Why was it such a big deal for him at that moment? Weren't we all in the punk underground because we were all different, and because none of us felt like we really belonged out there? It doesn't mean that you can't disagree on certain things.

I've been really hardcore antidrug from the get-go. I still am. Most of the people that I have loved in this world and most of the people that I have worked with through Positive Force—or anything that I have been involved with through the community—are folks that use drugs. I don't agree with it, but it doesn't stop me from loving them. I don't necessarily think that my way is the right way for everybody.

Of course, chaos ensues at Tim Kerr from the Big Boys' house with a big standoff with MDC. They supposedly vandalized Tim's house and essentially stole money because Biscuit had gotten pot for the band and was supposed to be paid back. Instead of getting the money back, there is a pile of weed ashes inside this long screed the Bad Brains left behind, telling Biscuit why he is going to burn in hell.

There's the two Josephs. Somehow, one of them is in the world of love and light, and the other is just lost somewhere in the darkness and full of something poisonous.

IAN MACKAYE

That situation with the Big Boys and all that in Austin was just fucked up, a mess. We were friends with the Big Boys, and thought they were a great band and great people. The fact that they got ripped off sucked. But it was especially terrible for me 'cause it was the Bad Brains going across the country. We were all excited that people would finally get to see the Bad Brains, and then we get the news that they ripped off the Big Boys. It was just madness at that time. They were on a different tip. Some of the people they were hanging with were scary dudes. There was probably some kind of commerce. Somebody was selling something, and there were definitely weapons involved. I had some very weird experiences with the people hanging around the band. I didn't always feel safe around those guys. They weren't interested in being friends with me, as much as they were interested in what I could provide perhaps. They would put up with me.

JOHN STABB

This stuff was negative and ignorant. It was hypocritical for H.R. to be doing these things. He would hang out and talk to us punk rock kids in his normal tone, and then he would totally change over to this Rastafarian thing with his Rasta friends, and he would just dismiss us. I had friends who were just like, "Get the fuck away from me," when he was around his Rastafarian friends. I thought it was kind of fake at the time. I thought he put on two different faces: one for the punk rock side of the population, and then he put on the other face for the Rastafarians. It really bothered me.

ANTHONY COUNTEY

It was problematic from the beginning with me and the band because of some of the Rasta influence. There were a lot of different influences. I didn't get to know the New York Rastas, really. They were not interested in knowing me, so I did not know them. There were influences that H.R. was under that I did not have direct contact with. I don't know what it was that they thought they needed to do, or what influence they had.

MARK ANDERSEN

The conviction that H.R. had— and I don't mean conviction like, oh, this is the right way—no, he meant revolution is coming. Babylon will fall. Ronald Wilson Reagan had just been elected president. What were the whispers in the Rasta community about Ronald Wilson Reagan? 666! Ronald Wilson Reagan: that's the full name of the president elected in the fall of 1980 and inaugurated in 1981. Ronald Wilson Reagan: six-letter first name, six letters in the middle name and six letters in the last name. 6-6-6. The antichrist, the beast in the Book of Revelations, which is a tremendously important book in Rasta theology. If you look at interviews at the time, H.R. absolutely believed revolution was coming and that they were part of it. It was going to be carried out by the youth. Somehow or another, they were in this place where they were helping to bring about this cosmic transformation, not just a political thing or spiritual thing. It's the righteous struggle of the oppressed against the oppressive. Scholars will tell you it's code for Nero. The emperor of Rome at the time was fiercely persecuting Christians. It was their coded way of saying Nero is going to fall, Rome is going to fall. Babylon as they knew it was going to fall. It's been used and reused and reinterpreted through centuries by many different oppressed groups who are hoping for the times when the first will be last and the last will be first. A cosmic reversal of the tables. At that moment, that's what H.R. believed was going to happen.

So you had this tremendous sense of mission and focus, and then it runs into messy reality in the form of the Castro in San Francisco, and the San Francisco punk scene's comfort with gays and lesbians. Then on top of that, what happens in Austin with the Big Boys. H.R. said in interviews at the time: "In order to be hardcore, it seemed like you had to be gay." That's what he took away from it. Whatever else you say about that, and I will say many critical things, that tour fundamentally changed H.R.'s attitude towards the punk community, and he didn't want to be part of it anymore. I believe he said, "Punk music is the devil's music," and he started announcing in interviews across the country that Bad Brains are going to disband at of the end of 1982, and an entity called Zion Train is going to take its place. It's the same people according to H.R., but the difference is they're

going to play only reggae music. They have been mixing reggae and punk, but it was going to become all reggae. What's missing in this scenario? No one else in Bad Brains had agreed to this.

H.R.

At that time, it was requested of us to play more punk rock songs. We wanted to play more reggae songs. By playing more reggae songs, I was able to express myself in a nicer and more humble way and be received that way. But the kids said, "No, man, we'd like you guys to play everything. It makes your shows more thrilling and more exciting, and it's not a bore." A lot of the kids had already seen reggae bands, but they never saw four black dudes playing a kind of music that was mostly introduced and delivered by Europeans, so they wanted to see us mainly for that reason. That's what led us eventually to, quote-unquote, fortune and fame.

MARK ANDERSEN

Darryl and Gary took pride in the hybrid they had created. They didn't want to be just a reggae band. They love doing reggae, but they were Bad Brains. They were something that blew these boundaries apart, and they would lose all of that if they just went reggae. They had built an audience as Bad Brains, and you could say there's a principle. The tour had gone badly in certain ways, and there would be this continuing recrimination against them for some of the stuff that happened on the tour. Fundamentally, though, even the people who disliked Bad Brains as people, who didn't agree with their politics, could not deny that they were about the best band that anyone had ever seen in that genre. If you go back there, you start to see not only the disintegration in the unity of the band, but I also think H.R.'s reaction seems more than simple homophobia. It seems like a symptom of something deeper and more worrisome. Like something is not quite solid in his psyche.

JOHN STABB

I think ever since Henry Rollins did Black Flag, he definitely got a little out there and weird, and I stopped supporting Black Flag at that point. I'm just a really critical person as far as things like that. But I think that Henry, over the years, has become really repentant about a lot of that stuff and has become a more likable person because of it. I do my ups-and-downs with H.R., too, but I just keep hearing more and more stuff. If he really came out and said something about it like, "I wish I hadn't done all those things," then I would totally give him credit, and I would be like, "Okay."

H.R.

At that time, it was very much about Rasta, hardcore Rasta, and what I understood from becoming a member of the 12 Tribes. It was basically very strict Christianity, but we called it Rasta. Today, I am much more live-and-let-live. I would not say those things today. I think age and experience changed me. We went from teen adults or juveniles to authentic adults, so our music changed. Our ideas changed along with our philosophy, and responding to things in a more responsible, mature and adult way. And

what we thought at the time when we were young was just old-fashioned, old ideas. But now, through experience, I've learned that it's better to use those laws and those teachings to make one's efforts more reasonable.

ANTHONY COUNTEY

Back then, he didn't trust the people that he was working with. He didn't trust me, I don't think. We were touring the country in a vehicle that we could barely pay for and, for the most part, people weren't showing up. Somewhere in there, Ric Ocasek saw them play and had the same reaction I did. Ric was really smart, and he was paying attention to things. He had been working with Suicide and other bands that were really phenomenal. It wasn't like he was a fake in any way at all. He'd been involved in some of the most important underground stuff in New York.

He wanted Bad Brains to come and record an album in Boston. They were at a point where they had enough material for an album, so that became *Rock for Light*. Before the record was even released, H.R. wanted to know where his money was. We didn't even have a label yet. Eventually, *Rock for Light* just got an indie release. PVC Records were about the only choice. There was never a million dollars, but H.R. thought that there was.

At one point, I had gotten fairly close to getting the band signed at Elektra Records. That would've been very good. They were really good people and were ready for something exciting, something new. H.R. blew it up. The A&R guy, Tom Zutaut, signed Guns N' Roses and a lot of great bands. We were out in LA and I had him out there with the band. H.R. basically didn't trust him or something and kind of gave him this rough vibe about messing with Rasta. After the meeting, Tom turned to me and said, "Anthony, I'm not sure, but did I just get my life threatened for trying to sign this band?" That's what pretty much finished that one. The thing that was so confusing to me was that H.R. thought there was money around when the deal actually didn't get done. He knew the deal didn't get done. He sank the deal. We never talked about what kind of money it could have meant.

H.R.

I didn't think accepting those exclusive deals at such low advances of funds would be cost-effective, so for that reason I decided to stray away from those deals and take my time and do research first. I didn't want to be exploited. I wanted to make sure I was doing the right thing, meaning playing the right kind of music and having the right kind of message, the proper message. It was important to be correct and upright professionally.

IAN MACKAYE

I remember sitting with H.R. and Darryl on my parents' porch and just talking, and H.R. saying, "Don't ever sign a contract. Don't ever put your name on a piece of paper. Don't ever sign nothing, no contracts. Only sign one if they're giving you a million dollars cash." I was like, "Okay. Makes sense to me. Fuck the man! No contracts."

7. HUMAN RIGHTS 1983–1985

I loved the sound of reggae music. It was beautiful to the ear, and was uplifting, and a better way to get Jah's message across to the youth without them getting beat up in the audience.

-H.R.

MARK ANDERSEN

Around 1983, when the rest of Bad Brains don't want to abandon punk rock music, there are serious problems. Tom Zutaut is the guy who signed Guns N' Roses, and he wanted to sign Bad Brains, so this war inside the band comes to a head the day Tom Zutaut comes to meet them. Zutaut knocks on the door. Joseph welcomes him in kindly, walks up to Darryl and says, "Darryl, I'd like you to meet Satan. Satan, this is Darryl." He's calling Tom Zutaut the devil!

For the band, this was outrageous. They're living in Alphabet City, they're getting married, they're starting to have kids. It's like, *Why should we not be able to live off this? We can still make the music pure. We can make it real. We don't want you fucking everything up!* The deal never came to pass, which was a multimillion-dollar deal, according to what I was told by Anthony Countey. So H.R. splits. He and Earl returned to DC and left the other two there. I think there's bitterness from that that has never healed, because they were at the edge of breaking through, and Joseph threw it away.

I don't know exactly when Joseph officially joins the 12 Tribes of Israel up in New York, but it's clear that his faith is the center of his life. It was a struggle between the church and the roadhouse basically—the struggle between God and the devil within the eyes of many in the African-American community. He takes on a new name, Joseph I, and he begins to view things as punk versus reggae: reggae being gospel music and punk being the devil's music. I think this is the real drama of this search for Joseph I: Who is Paul Hudson? Who is H.R.? It's partly about the extinguishing of this extraordinary artistic gift, but it's also something much more important than that. This life of this incredible person with such kindness and generosity, who sees his life is on the line.

KENNY DREAD

I lived with H.R. the winter after he split from the Bad Brains, and I saw somebody who was resting after four years on the front lines of a war. It was like one thrash after another for four years at maximum intensity. Eventually the human body has to rest. The soul has to rest. They knocked down the walls of Babylon over those years from 1979 to 1983, constantly touring.

SAUL WILLIAMS

There are so many ways to destroy Babylon. Malcolm X had a book deal through Alex Haley, where he received an advance to meet with Alex Haley on a regular basis to discuss his life and sculpt that beautiful autobiography. At the same time, the deal was with a corporate entity, so how do you navigate that? That's what we all have been trying to figure out.

AL ANDERSON

Joseph was always concerned with giving off the appearance of selling out. He believed that if you sign to these major labels, they will take away your creativity and tell you what to play or how to write songs. He wanted to keep his independence. I think that was the biggest conflict; he wanted to be his own man. He didn't want to be a yes-man to no record company or be obligated to jump through hoops or whatever, to be a revolutionary-type performer. I believe in my heart this is why people think he was throwing monkey wrenches into the plans. The other band members knew he didn't really want to continue the punk thing. H.R. felt that the band should have outgrown that, because reggae is a much more ancient and mature form of music. He felt like, "Yeah, we were young, but we're older now, let's represent. We all are Rasta. Darryl is a Rasta. Dr Know is a Rasta. Earl is a Rasta. Let's be more reflective of what we look like, or what we say and we represent." Punk really wasn't the avenue to reflect who he was or what he represented in terms of the Rastafari movement.

MICHAEL FRANTI

Rasta has played a really important role in music over the years. You see all different types of Rasta being presented that are from a certain order or discipline or a certain tribe. Then you have some where it's just like a style, or

a hairstyle, or a name, or red, gold and green put on the cover of a record or whatever, and that's as deep as it goes. For a lot of us, Bob Marley was the only thing we knew about Rasta, and we had never seen an American talking about repatriation or talking about Marcus Garvey or talking about Haile Selassie. There was this empowerment of black people that was connected to Africa. Rasta was always about connecting to God. Something that was eternal. Something that was greater than yourself.

H.R.

The 12 Tribes of Israel is a religious foundation grounded and founded on the beautiful island of Jamaica. It is based on there being twelve sons in the Bible: Reuben, Naphtali, Benjamin, Simeon, Judah, Levi, Issachar, Zebulun, Dan, Gad and Asher. That's how it goes, and in between all that, there is Joseph, which is the tribe I'm from. Bob Marley was Joseph, too. A lot of it is inspired by the Holy Bible and the Scriptures.

One day, some brothers came and shared a pamphlet with me, a little flier that was beautiful, and it had a picture of Haile Selassie on it. That's when I started to do some research on Haile Selassie, and I said, "Yeah, man, that's the ticket." And that's when I started to leave all those drugs alone.

I had heard that playing reggae music attracted decent people, and I wanted to attract those people. I had a belief that although it may not be the end of the world, it's going to be the end of all "isms" and "schisms." We had to have a place where we could go and lift our souls up. I asked where they were located, and one of them said, "You'll find it bredren," and then he just turned around and walked away. It was before my dreadlocks years when I was a bald-head youth. I eventually went to New York and located one of the homes that they would have their meetings at on a regular basis.

Yes I. Make a joyful noise unto the Lord of all the land. Serve the Lord with gladness. Come before His presence with vocalizing. Know the Lord; He is God. It is He who had made them and not themselves. We are His people and the sheep of His pasture. Enter unto His courts with praise, and be thankful unto Him. Come before the presence of the Lord, for He is God. He had made Himself. Be thankful and praise His name. Bless His people for the Lord is good, very good. His mercy is everlasting, and His truth endures for all generations. I want to thank the Almighty One.

JULIAN CAMBRIDGE

Dude, he could have found Buddhism or anything else, but it was what was happening at that time in the world. It was Rasta time. At one time it was afro time, but then it was Rasta time. And we all became targets as long as we were Rasta back then. *How much guns you got? Where's the weed? Take your hat off, blah blah blah.* That's how the police dealt with us then. It happened to me a lot. It happens a lot still. It's just America. Ain't nothing changed.

AL ANDERSON

He was always talking about the street, real people in the struggle. Rasta. Poverty . . . degradation. Being looked at low because of your hairstyle or maybe your diet, but I think he transcended so much more energy beyond that. When you're going through changes as a singer-songwriter, you start thinking and writing about the reality in your own world and what's around you, and after a while, you come to a conclusion about your own reality.

H.R.

The Brains did a show once with Peter Tosh over in Stony Brook University, and for the first three or four songs, people said, "What are these dudes playing?" And around the fifth song, we played reggae and everybody got up and started clapping. So I knew then that in order to reach people on that level, we would have to do something that they could identify with, and that was when we authentically became the vehicle, the chariot that the masses could relate to. We decided that Bad Brains were going to take a spiritual retreat, and do a little soul-searching, and get to know ourselves, and do a little research into the religion. So we decided that Bad Brains would disband, and we would go our separate ways.

I wanted to come up with a nice, clear message and a way to present our tunes in a more professional and proper way. I began to research my Scriptures and the beautiful brothers and sisters of the 12 Tribes hipped me to what was really going on in the world. It was something to think about, because while a lot of people were sleeping, it was time to wake up. I could either sleep my life away or go out there and do something about it, and that's what I did.

JIMMY GESTAPO

When he got deep into the Rasta thing, he used to stroll down St. Mark's Place with a staff. He was cocksure and positive and focused. When he talked to you, he was engaging and he'd look you in the eye when you were talking to him. H.R. was strong, powerful, healthy and just badass. It was like, *Holy shit, Jah is coming down the block. Look out!* He was going through a very powerful time, and a lot of people got into it, including myself. Everybody was trying to grow dreadlocks. Everybody was saying "boss" and talking the way Rastas talk. It definitely became—I don't know about it being a trendy thing—but an influence thing. Hipsters are trendy; reggae is spiritual. It doesn't have to be a thing of color. It definitely taught people about Ital food. I think a lot of good came from it. And reggae definitely chilled a lot of crazy kids out at a time when we were listening to some pretty aggro music. It was nice to have reggae to cool out to. It saved a lot of people's heads from getting cracked.

H.R.

I found a reason to record and jam again. Reggae music
sounded much more pleasant and I love that sound. That's
one thing about Bob Marley: he could play some good music,
and his sound was so massive and harmonious, and that
attracted me. I decided to start my own group, Zion Train.

ANTHONY COUNTEY

H.R. had different ideas. He wanted to end Bad Brains and
launch Zion Train. Since there had been another band
called Zion Train, they were only Zion Train for maybe a
moment, maybe one show. He would do things like that. He
would announce something from the stage, and I would be,
like, "You're kidding, right? This is your last show?" Some
things I couldn't take him seriously. I was trying to function
in their interest and not let them hurt themselves.

KENNY DREAD

In the early days, H.R. and Bad Brains' embrace of Rastafari
became a divisive situation in the punk rock community.
The entire audience would sometimes leave the club when
they would break into the reggae songs, and it took a long
time for this spirituality to permeate and be respected. It
was disturbing to me personally. I was first attracted to H.R.
not through the thrash, I was attracted to the reggae and
H.R.'s singing.

RAS MICHAEL | SONS OF NEGUS

When me and H.R. met, me say, "Bad Brains: what ya' talk
about Bad Brains? Good Brains! Jah Brains! That is the
brain you have to deal with now. Good Brains, God Brains,
not Bad Brains. You jump on the crowd of people, and what
if people jump out of the way? You jump on the asphalt or
the concrete and hurt yourself." I talk direct to him, and
him dissect the words and see the trueness in that. We

don't want nothing bad, man. Everything for good. What is badness? Badness brings sadness. Love brings happiness. Love and happiness—that's what you have to deal with. Look upon yourself. Look how Jah make you: handsome, nice. Give Him a good voice so that you can sing of His praises.

COREY GLOVER

You can hear it in the lyrics that he's trying to get an understanding of God and how God works. Some people get very close, and I think he's one person who has gotten very close to understanding what God is. When H.R.'s able to express himself and you hear him and it comes through him and he throws it back up as a praise to his higher power, it's a powerful thing. It's amazing to watch and amazing to aspire to.

MARK ANDERSEN

H.R. the performer is still obviously extraordinary. He started the H.R. Band and Human Rights, which were actually pretty accomplished and did pretty well within the reggae world. He got the right people around him and, you know, they're trying to be Bob Marley and the Wailers. Human Rights is walking in the shadows of giants, but they're doing okay. As an artist, he's still got that spark.

EARL HUDSON

Darryl and Doc, those cats became nailed into New York by that time. They started having kids and they were cemented into New York and weren't leaving, and that's when H left. I stayed up there for a little while to see if we could get the shit back together with Bad Brains, and it didn't happen. So I was, like, "I got to head on back home." And so me and Joe started Human Rights and started playing reggae. We got some cats together and started to get that music together.

H.R.

I was kind of versatile and universal, and although the Brains did exist, Human Rights was brand new. It was a new style a new technique. I wanted to venture off and just give it a try, and be able to use the styles and techniques I learned from reggae and apply it to my music. That's what I did.

MARK ANDERSEN

It began as a little more rock than punk, and there is certainly reggae, but it's not that far from Bad Brains. It's the Joseph who's in military fatigues. He's ready for the revolution. Bad Brains won't do it, so this is the band that's going to do it. The title of one of the songs he wrote upon his return to DC is "Let's Have a Revolution."

AL "JUDAH" WALKER

It was late 1983, early 1984: The "Dread House," as it was called, was at 1700 17th Street, right across from the Third District police department. H.R. moved into this three-level house, and basically all the roommates were musicians. Kenny Dread had a go-go group called Outrage. There were a few other people who were basically punk rock kids just camping out to have somewhere to live, and then there was me. I think Joe was at his heights at the Dread House. He dressed in camouflage almost every day. Basically, we just lived and rehearsed music there and talked about politics and the Bible, ate Ital food and smoked ganja, and gave thanks to Jah. It was a good atmosphere. Joe felt pretty much at home and comfortable there. When I think back, those were pretty much the best days.

SKEETER THOMPSON | SCREAM

I lived there with my ex-wife and the other roommates: Julie Bird and Kenny Dread, and I think Banks was there, too. I can't remember, but, anyway, H.R. lived there, and he had the smallest room in the whole house. You could almost touch the walls extending your arms out. It had a bed in there and a little round table. I think it was one of those spools. You know, you can wrap wire on it, but it was maybe two–and–a–half–feet high, and he put a smock over it, or some sort of colorful cloth, and it was just his Bible on top of it. And it's the strangest thing, because that's when I really got to know the man. There were times I would walk by and hear him crying like he was going through some sort of torment. I would hear him talking to himself. I always thought he was praying out loud. He was always partaking. He was always breaking bread. It was always covert. It wasn't, like, "Let's go get high" or "Let's have a session," and we began reasoning. He started growing locks. They all started growing locks. He wanted to be called Joseph at that time. Before, H.R. stood for "Hunting Rod" because he was such a ladies' man. At least that's the way that I perceived it. He would go out there and just go hunting, trying to find some pussy. I remember we were having a reasoning session, and I was like, "Are you going to call your band H.R.? Doesn't that stand for Human Rights?" He was real quiet, and about twenty minutes later, we were talking about something else, and he was like, "Yeah, man, Human Rights. That's it. That's what we're going to call it."

KENNY DREAD

Our community was like an ashram, and H.R. was our guru. The spiritual vibe permeated the Dread House. H.R. is a shaman. H.R. was a teacher every moment there was an opportunity for a lesson. Being powerful and capable and being the best, but being humble about it was an amazing lesson.

H.R.

I heard that being on the self-sufficient tip and having your own record company was where it was at, because then one could control their destiny, so I decided to start Olive Tree Records. I took it upon myself to seal up the confirmation, an agreement that I made with the church and God. Up until then, this was all just a thought, but a new movement was being started, and there were a bunch of kids that knew what was going on. They understood and they felt the same way, and they wanted to be a part of the new style of living and the new approach. We believed that although money was around, one shouldn't make it the focal point of the group, but use it as an assistant to achieve what one wants to achieve. Find a richness of one's soul and character and personality, and once you've done that, you'll have a better perspective on life, and you'll be able to use what God has given you: your natural-born talent to succeed in life.

SKEETER THOMPSON

I remember he had the least amount of complaints out of the whole group, and he used the least amount of energy—water and food. And he was always there to help out. He actually wanted the doors to be left open. You live in DC, you don't want to do that, but in the daytime, he wanted to leave them open. He was suggesting things like that. People were like, No. At the time, it was, you know, the murder capital, and it was just hot with drugs and sex. And 14th Street was full of hookers and strip joints. It was real dangerous, a fast and spontaneous place.

JIMI RILEY | OLIVE TREE RECORDS

He was trying to motivate us to be Jah youth. That's what the Tree was called before it became Olive Tree; it was called Jah Youth. He was mocking Hitler Youth. He had a weird thing where he would talk about Hitler a lot and how he manipulated the crowd through his use of films and music. He would have his little ranting Bible meetings at the house, which used to crack me up because he would sit in a room, they would all smoke little joints, and he would almost be goose-stepping while he would read from the Bible. He would chastise them to be better people and tell them what they had to do to help God come to America and bring down Babylon. And they would all do the "blood clot, bumba clot" and all their little pet words. He always had his Bible with him, and his little crate with his rolling papers to roll his spliffs. I would come home to the house, and I knew he was at the house because he had this weird way of drawing in and smoking. He would chant and read from the Bible. It was very unusual.

JOSE GONZALES | HUMAN RIGHTS, THE MOB

All of us smoked copious amounts of herb. It was a part of our daily life. Not once a day, not twice a day, but many,

many times a day. At that time, it was just based on the Rastafarian religion. We were smoking together as a group of friends: a group of people with like minded goals, ideals and religious beliefs.

KENNY DREAD

Julie Bird came from this incredibly illustrious family, and yet she had a real iconoclastic streak of her own. She had followed the Grateful Dead. She had watched her father sit there and communicate with Russian paranormal scientists before the Cold War was over. She was a rebel in her own way. She was a bit older than us, and she came from money. It was a situation where we needed the partner in our record company to help us pay the bills and help us press these records. She was also just completely addicted to the music. So in short order, we became a family and she became like our sugar mama—but also like a sister and a real friend.

AL "JUDAH" WALKER

She's the cofounder of Olive Tree Records, and she produced the first Zion Train LP. She also resided at the Dread House. She was instrumental financially in producing the first few H.R. projects and getting them off the ground.

JULIE BIRD | OLIVE TREE RECORDS

The 17th and U house, the Dread House, became Olive Tree House, because Olive Tree Records was developed there. At the time, we were doing a lot of productions. We had very deep negations with the 12 Tribes and musicians in the reggae scene in DC at the time, and it was a very suspicious time. We were a group with a productive purpose, and yet I think a model of collective living most people did not trust. We were able to produce and publish and distribute and pay bills.

H.R.

A lot of it was inspired by the Holy Bible and the Scriptures and also by authentic Rastafarians and other good-hearted people who are not really Rasta, but from their hearts, they are delivered from the spirit of God within. And their support to me was overwhelming and a big, big blessing. The same way the spirit works, you plant a seed in the fertile soil, and it's just a matter of time before it blossoms and becomes a fruit, and we're getting paid from the fruit of our labor.

It was a complete universal objective where we would read our Bibles and still use the same techniques in our music. I didn't want anybody to be misled. I was still working on whether or not I should be a supporter of that punk style of music. I thought, *Don't worry 'bout a thing. As long as you're being yourself and you're being honest, the truth will shine like a light.* And I said to myself, "I don't really know if I'm going to be ready for that kind of changeover, but I will give it a try." And much to my surprise, it was received well by the audience. It really didn't matter, punk versus reggae, as long as we got onstage and jammed.

JIMI RILEY

I met H.R. because I was at the Dread House, as they called it, at 17th and U and started buying weed from H.R. one day. I said, "Hey, I've always been a fan and I love 'Pay to Cum,' and I'd love to do some artwork for you." That's when he opened the door and let me come in. He gave me this stick drawing of the H.R. logo and said, "I want you to turn it into something. I want people to be reminded of a classic rock band logo like AC/DC and KISS." We started hanging, and we would talk about religion and God, and we'd smoke ganja and just talk. I wanted to move downtown because I was living with my parents and going to Northern Virginia Community College studying graphic art. They wanted me to move in there, and the rent was only like $900 a month, so I figured, divided by a bunch of people, we would have really cheap rent. It became the headquarters for Olive Tree Records. Anyway, H.R. figured out I was gay. He asked me, and I said, "Yes." He said, "You are a faggot! God does not want you," and he just slammed the door and stormed off. I thought Rastafarian meant more than that, and you didn't get grounded down in these petty things. H.R. just shut down and wouldn't even look at me and wouldn't talk to me anymore. We had gotten along great and did all this stuff. I was their roadie, and we hung out. Suddenly, he couldn't be my friend even though we were good friends up until then. I was heartbroken.

IAN MACKAYE

There were some good moments, but it seemed like it largely centered on getting high. There was a whole part of the scene that was just caught up in that Olive Tree world, which was a different clique altogether. I think they thought we at Dischord were too straight. They thought, *You guys aren't doing it right. You're not doing publishing, you're not doing contracts and managers.* But that just wasn't our thing. We were never interested in any of that. The impression I got from the Olive Tree people was that they were going to operate it like a "real" label, whatever that means. They had some cool releases. I thought the first H.R. record was all right and the Beefeater Need a Job EP was great, but ultimately I don't think anybody was really minding the store. All of this was happening at a time that there were lot of people who seemed like lost kids gravitating around H.R. I'm not sure what they were looking for, maybe it was mostly about getting high, but in any event I think it lent to his sense of being a shepherd.

JOSE GONZALES

To my understanding, the H.R. project started in New York. The very first incarnation of the H.R. band came about because the Bad Brains were having issues amongst themselves and they weren't getting along at the time. The first incarnation didn't get out of the rehearsal studio in New York City. It was myself on bass; Gary Miller on guitar; David Hahn, who had been Bad Brains' manager for a short amount of time on drums; and H.R. on vocals. We rehearsed with the idea of doing a couple of one-off gigs in California. That didn't work out for whatever reason. We couldn't get it together. H.R. decided to bring the entire project to Washington, DC. He wanted to get together with local musicians that he knew. David Byers specifically was a key factor, and he was one of the first names mentioned by H.R. He wanted to work with David, who was an incredibly talented guitar player and songwriter. On second guitar was David Jordan, another very talented guitar player, and Earl on drums. He asked me if I would be interested in relocating from New York to DC to work on this project. That is like asking a young Metallica fan if they want to come and join Metallica. So I thought about it for three quarters of a second and said, "Yes." I left everything in New York that I was doing, relocated to DC, and started rehearsing with them. We took a working-class approach to it. We rehearsed four to five times a week with the intention of doing something different. Not necessarily hardcore Bad Brains style, but he wanted to embrace different styles of music that were in his heart and in his brain. Consequently, we got together that first H.R. album, *It's About Luv*.

KENNY DREAD

The minute Earl showed up from New York, everything changed. H.R. was suddenly jumping up and operating, getting rehearsal spaces, organizing guitarists. Then Jose came down to play the bass; that's Jose Gonzalez, who was the bass player from the New York hardcore band The Mob. So now you have your rhythm section, and then H.R. added David Byers on the guitar and David Jordan, so the group began rehearsing at David Jordan's house. I began booking some gigs up and down the East Coast, and that was the first version of the H.R. band, Human Rights. Dave Byers was one

of the first African-American punk rockers in the DC scene. Same generation as Bad Brains, and same generation as Skeeter Thompson from Scream. We weren't just a band; we were a posse. We lived together, rocked together, conquered together. Our performances sometimes became like a basketball game, keeping score. Who had 'em dancing the most, who had 'em thrashing the most, who had 'em freakin' out the most. And we went out there to win every time. It was an incredible experience to play music with someone who lived it—one hundred percent rocker.

DAVID JORDAN | H.R. BAND

The only reason he hired me was because I had a place to rehearse. I charged him by the hour anyway. Gotta rehearse somewhere. And I played music twenty-four hours a day. Me and David Byers basically wrote all the music, then we had to show it to Jose from The Mob and Earl, and we'd just try to get it with no mistakes. Joe was just sitting down there writing with a pad, and he'd write the lyrics while we rehearsed the music, and by the time we could play the music without making too many mistakes, he'd written the lyrics. Then he started rehearsing *It's About Luv* with us. We wrote it and rehearsed it in about three weeks, I'd say, or less, and then we went and recorded it. Me and Earl did all of our tracks live, and Byers kept going in and erasing his parts and doing them over again. I used to smoke weed, and when I got to the studio, nobody's got pot except me. They supposed to be Rastamen and shit.

JOSE GONZALES

At the same time, he wanted to do an all-reggae project, which became the Zion Train band, and that was many musicians from different parts of the country and some locals. He knew some dreads there that were interested in playing with him. So Human Rights and Zion Train were actually two separate things. There was Human Rights, which was a little bit of hardcore, some reggae, some jazz/ pop and some regular pop. And then there was the all-reggae Zion Train with Al Judah on vocals. He was the main vocalist, H.R. was playing guitar, Earl was playing drums and we had a horn section. God, I think maybe we had nine people on stage. Initially, his intention was just to focus on the reggae band, but he also didn't want to alienate his fan base. I think he wanted to give them a little something, so he came up with the two-band concept. We're talking 1983– 84. He was just writing songs daily with David Byers's help. Earl, of course, was also contributing to the songwriting process, and it was amazing to watch him work.

AL "JUDAH" WALKER

It was my idea to have a group called Zion Train with me and Joe as the front men. The other guys wanted to play reggae, but they just wanted to do both—punk, too—so it was kind of pulling Joe. He did it to keep the band going and to keep everybody's livelihood, but you could tell in his heart that he always wanted to play roots music. My inspiration for Zion Train came from a Bob Marley song called "Zion Train." In the Rastafari faith, Zion is what people would call heaven,

so he related to that very strongly. He didn't want to play punk anymore because the more he read his Bible and kept company around other Rastas, he just felt the need to only play Jah music. He didn't really consider punk Jah music.

STEVEN HANNER | OLIVE TREE RECORDS PHOTOGRAPHER

Zion Train was a combo of a couple different bands but came out of these reasoning sessions at the Olive Tree House. The reasoning sessions were always about purpose. We were there to work together and to get on the right page. A bunch of us were dreading up and serious about it. The sessions were meetings of minds and spirits. Gigs got worked out, and calendars were organized along the way. We passed the Coptic Bible around, reading passages. That was the direction towards Zion Train. H.R. was becoming this guru, and there were a lot of followers showing up at the Dread House. A lot of friends and musicians attracted to him, and all of a sudden there was this very big band. David Byers might be playing guitar one time, and then there might be two or three other guitarists or a different bass player or different drummers. It was strictly Ital reggae.

JOSE GONZALES

Before each show there was always a prayer. We would huddle up and ask God for guidance to give us the strength and the will to play our instruments well, so that we could deliver this message in the proper fashion. That was very important in our daily life, not just onstage. Everything was focused on being together as human beings with one goal, which was Rastafari. Simple, that's what it was.

AL "JUDAH" WALKER

We did a big show at CBGB. It was Zion Train, and the other half of the show was H.R. Me and Joe were the front men. We did the Zion Train set first. The next set was H.R. It was a good mixture of music, about three or four punk jams, a few R & B-type songs and a nice tribute to his son: a happy birthday song, which is a nice reggae dub. "Happy Birthday My Son," like the beginning lyrics of the song: "May 23rd, 1984, I was on the corner looking for more, out comes Babylon to lock I up and throw away the key, I was only looking for some money to buy my son some pants, shirts and some shoes." He got caught selling herb that same day. That was in Adams Morgan. It happened to be his son P.J.'s birthday, so while he was in lockup, he composed that song, so when he came out, we all rehearsed it and he recorded it on the first H.R. album, *It's About Luv*.

MARK ANDERSEN

He's living in a communal house on 17th and U. And, you know, they're running a huge pot operation. Of course, H.R. gets himself arrested up on Columbia Road for dealing.

KENNY DREAD

Someone ran in and told us Joseph got arrested. I used to go buy weed from H.R. on the corner up on Columbia Road, near the Ontario Theatre. It was a way for someone in a band to make money, and it's all documented beautifully in "Happy Birthday My Son." Something that always amazed me was that you might have a really big gig one night, but you've still got to make money the next day selling marijuana. I made a part of my living this way back in the day. A lot of us did. It was sort of flexible income for a musician.

JIMI RILEY

I told him not to go on the street that day, "Just don't go. I think something's going to happen, plus you have a show tonight." He said, "I have to go. I need some money for one of my kids." I just knew something was going to happen that day, and then he went up on the block. I think within ten minutes of him being on the corner, they got him. And we didn't do the gig that night. We tried to do several benefits for him. We did a lot of shows at The Hung Jury and always put "Free H.R." on the fliers.

H.R.

At the time I was one of those gullible youths who believed whatever people were telling me. Like one day, somebody said, "Did you hear the good news? DC Jail's got a hotel and a club called DC Jail." I said, "No way!" I said, "Hold on, let's have a jam session at DC Jail." I actually thought in my heart that there was a jam session at the DC Jail. Anyway, P.J., my son, he was about seven or eight years old, and I would bring him around here and we'd walk around, go to some of the Ethiopian clubs and restaurants or up to Madam's Organ, where we did our first shows.

AL "JUDAH" WALKER

He found a lot of time when he wasn't on the road to spend with his son and to teach him things, and explain exactly who he was and what his goals were. He did all he could to stay connected with his son, Paul Jr.

KENNY DREAD

I definitely remember this beautiful gig my band Outrage played at DC Space, where H.R. guested on a few songs. P.J. was up there, I believe he was about seven years old at the time, and he was up there playing the tambourine. He was a great kid.

JULIE BIRD

We saw P.J. on various occasions when they had a coming together. He lived with us for a while. It's an unusual story: multiple women, multiple children. Remember Fela Kuti who had 278 wives in his independent nation, which was on the grounds of his property? He ran to be Nigerian president. He was H.R.'s peer.

KENNY DREAD

The first H.R. solo band gigs in '84 were supposed to be a national tour that was unfortunately cut short due to one of H.R.'s periods of incarceration. In 1988, we did a tour all over the States. '89 was Europe. In the early days, the reputation that was already established by Bad Brains made the whole East Coast available to us immediately. Some of the earliest gigs were in Philly, New York, North Carolina, Atlanta, and, of course, DC.

DAVID JORDAN

We had a seventeen-song set list, but we'd never play more than seven to eight songs 'cause Joe had in his contract: "If you can't control the crowd, the show is over." So he would incite the crowd as much as he could, and then when the crowd goes nuts and jumps all up on the stage, we'd just go off the stage and the show's over. I ain't gonna let people stomp all over my cords and shit and pull the plugs out of my amp. We were contracted to play fifty to seventy minutes, but we never played more than twenty-five because the crowd went wild.

CHUCK TREECE

I was in McRad at the time, and H.R. called my house and asked if we'd come down to DC and play a show. It was cool because we all looked up to H, and he was doing the first H.R. record. He borrowed my guitar for the show, so I kinda

tripped out at that. It was different than the Bad Brains because it was a bigger band, more like a Marley phase of what a punk rocker would do. It wasn't the traditional Jamaican musicians, it was everybody, all these friends of his from DC Dave Byers was a great guitar player, a neo-classical shredder. Maybe Dave listened to more metal growing up, because most guitar players that shred listen to way more metal than R & B. Earl was playing drums. That was my favorite band of H.R.'s as far as when he stepped out to do his own thing. I still wanted him to be the H.R. from the Bad Brains, but he was so into this other thing.

DAVID JORDAN

After the first couple of tour legs we did together, I was like *Man, I can't be cooped up in a van with this guy. I'm gonna hurt him. I'm gonna hit him in the head with a hatchet or something, because he don't know how to act.* Like one time, he kept messing with the bass player's mother, and I was, like, "This is one of your band members' mother. Don't try to fuck her! Leave her alone." I was about to hit him in the head with a hatchet. This was the last straw.

WILLIAM BANKS

I experienced a lot of things with H.R., good times and bad. H.R. used to be a physical person. I don't know why, but he used to get physical and stuff with the band members. Maybe too much talking. We were on the road. You know, talking so much stuff—gibberish. You get to a point where you're just talking nonsense, and sometimes it might hurt somebody's feelings and you get tired of it. The road . . . for some people might get you upset. Somebody's feet might be stinking and smelling the whole time. You might not say something for a while, and the next thing you know, you blow up. I did some stuff where he blew up, but it's all good. Calmed down and kept moving on. You've got to know how to deal with people when you're around them. You've got to know what buttons to push and what buttons you don't push.

MARK ANDERSEN

He did create Zion Train and Human Rights, but you get a sense that something is not quite connecting. I mean, there's a recording of Zion Train, and even though Joseph connected with other gifted musicians like Dave Byers to play guitar in Human Rights, it wasn't Bad Brains. It was good, and it had an audience, but he needed Darryl and Gary. Earl, Darryl and Gary together—you know, you can't touch them. That terrific focus that Joseph has is starting to waver. A lot of us didn't understand what was happening, but as unfortunate and ugly things began to happen around Joseph personally, it started to become clear that there were perhaps other factors at play. Now it's around 1985, basically a year and a half of being apart, Bad Brains reunite their original lineup and they're just as great as they ever were. In fact, if you listen to *I Against I*, the album that comes out of that reunited Bad Brains, it's arguably the most realized and influential work that they did because they started bringing stuff together, also adding a little more metal. They had something. It was like the magic was back.

8. RETURN TO HEAVEN 1985–1987

I regretted not really being around the group as much because we were musically at a high point in our careers, and a lot of things were happening. While I was away, the band was getting offers from different record labels and I wasn't around. I just didn't want to be exploited.
-H.R.

ANTHONY COUNTEY

Chris Williamson was a promoter in New York, and he was promoting shows at something called the Rock Hotel on Jane Street, a real hole in the wall. He was launching this venue and he asked, "Do you think you can give me the Bad Brains?" It was 1985, and at that point Doc and Darryl weren't really involved. It wound up being just a matter of a couple phone calls. They got together, rehearsed, and basically, the rehearsal turned into writing the record *I Against I*. Most of that record was composed in preparation for those shows. So when they got onstage and played those Rock Hotel shows, it was like Bad Brains were back. It was all really amazing.

IAN MACKAYE

I Against I was a real shift, a hugely influential record in terms of the music. Fugazi had started practicing around the time that record came out. Those songs were a little more rhythm-oriented and it felt like a liberating record. When they went to New York, they got super fast, and it was just crazy sounding, so it struck me as a significant departure when *I Against I* came out.

NICK HEXUM

I was in my junior year of high school in Omaha in 1987, and my skinhead friend was like, "If you like punk and you like reggae, you've got to hear Bad Brains." I had been really into The Clash and Bob Marley. This was well before the Internet, and it took a while to find out about different bands. Anyway, this guy was playing me the ROIR sessions, and I became obsessed with Bad Brains.

To hear the progression and change going into *I Against I* further blew my mind. I would get into these hypnotic bike rides with my Walkman where I would just listen to *I Against I*, really experiencing that music. It was life-changing for me to hear the jazz fusion sounds with metal. Looking at the liner notes and seeing Ron St. Germain was the producer, I said, "Wow, these drums sound so good and everything just sounds so crisp." It was like an explosion in my frontal lobe. When I hooked up with the guys that eventually became 311, we were really into the production on Bad Brains, so it was one of our dreams to work with Ron St. Germain.

ANTHONY COUNTEY

I went to Alan Douglas because I wanted an engineer who was capable of being a producer. I had to get somebody for a reasonable price who knew what the fuck they were doing. Alan turned me on to Ron St. Germain because Ron had been the engineer for some of Alan's Hendrix work. SST was the only label that even wanted to put the record out because the band had gotten kind of a rough name.

RON ST. GERMAIN

I was in the middle of mixing one of the Duran Duran offshoot records called Arcadia, which was one of the highest budget albums I had ever worked on. At the end of the day, it was probably $1.2 million, and it was during that project that I received a cassette. I listened to this cassette, and I was like, *Are you kidding me?* It was of a live performance of the Bad Brains. When I heard the music, I had to go see them. They were playing at the Ritz, so I squeezed out a night and ran down there and was completely flabbergasted. It was even better than the cassette. I thought, *Man this is outrageous. Definitely, absolutely, I'm in.* I definitely wanted to do it.

After I saw the band, I called up Greg Ginn at SST. I said, "I love the band, man. This is amazing. What have you got to make the record?" He said, "We will give you $5,000." And I said, "Well, which song do you want to do?" He said, "No, no, no, no. That's for the whole album." I said, "Really?" He said, "That's what we do, man." It was SST. They have all these starving bands. It's this indie, underground label. I said, "Okay, no problem. I'll do it."

I had been doing a lot of work up in Massachusetts at Longview Farm since the '70s. It was a really impressive place, a 150-year-old farm on ninety acres or something like that. Just a great place to take a band where you got them out of their environment. You all lived there, they fed you, they washed your clothes and they adjusted their schedule to you. I said this is what we need 'cause this is gonna be really intense. I could get three days for 4,500 bucks, so I took them up there.

I remember when H.R. first walked into the house and the studio, he was kind of floating, and he says, "I have arrived. I have arrived." My original thought going up there was to do this

live to two-track, because these guys were so unbelievable live. I didn't know any other band, particularly in the rock world or that hardcore world, that even had the balls to do that. I said, "This band has what it takes to do that," and since we didn't have any budget, we kind of had to.

So that first day, everyone was set up, and the drums were not sounding good. We only had three days, so we sent somebody from the studio to Boston to rent a different set and bring it back. That was sixty miles there and back, so we rehearsed in the meantime, and I set the guitars up and the basses up and did all of that. In the barn they could stand on the stage and perform as a band, which was good and I kind of got levels for the two-track. The vocals were so demanding, unbelievably demanding. We were having to do five or six takes, which with a normal song, probably wouldn't be that hard, but I could see H.R.'s voice going down really quick. I had to drop back and punt. I said, "Okay, we're gonna have to go to tape, and I'll have to mix this later." So we put up that 24-track, and during the day, I was patching things around, getting all the individual sounds together. New drums came in the next day, so we went for it.

What we would do is get a track, get happy with it, and then H.R. would give a reference vocal. We went through it that way until we got all the songs, and then it was Sunday and we were still working. I think it was around noon or so, and we didn't really have the vocals the way we should, so we put H.R. in the house studio with Phil Burnett, who was engineering with me back then. We set up the sounds there, and I said, "Just give me two full takes all the way down, all the way through of everything we've got."

They finished up about the time we finished up, and H.R. tells me, "Man, we gotta get these vocals, 'cause I've got to go to jail tomorrow." "What?! Now you're telling me?!"

He only had time to get a couple of takes 'cause he had somebody coming to get him to bring him to jail. Somehow he just nailed it down, and we got everything done except "Sacred Love."

H.R.

Some dudes were telling me once that by smoking herb and selling herb, it would be a one-way ticket to the big time. Well, it was my ticket to one of the deadliest places you could think of and it was called DC Jail. I had been selling a few bags when I had gotten back, and I called my brother to come to pick me up. One night, they pulled us over, and there was a whole bunch of marijuana in teeny bags. It wasn't a picnic in there, and there wasn't much to do except sit there and wait until your time is up.

EARL HUDSON

We was hustling, man. Trying to eat food, you know. You can't play music and work at damn Walmart. You've got to do something, so yeah, you get caught up sometimes. We were getting ready to go on tour in Providence, Rhode Island, so I went to pick Joe up. He put the runnings under the seat. I think somebody busted on us 'cause we came to a red light, and all of a sudden, the lights of the police car came on and they went right under his seat. It was my car, so that's why I had to go to jail, but he primarily caught the beef for that 'cause it was underneath the seat he was sitting on. We were in DC Jail together, and that's when we were pretty much finishing up that album. They wanted him to finish up the vocals on "Sacred Love," so somehow or another, it got hooked up and recorded. My dad was a correctional officer. He was a captain, and two of his sons are in jail. He never came to see us because my dad's a former soldier and he don't play that shit, but he'd have his friend in there bring me some cigarettes, and he must have had something or other to do with recording him in the jail.

ANTHONY COUNTEY

H.R. was an orderly in there. He got to clean up after lunch or something like that. He told me that the mess hall was not connected to the rest of the place. There was a phone in there and based on the layout, no one would be able to hear him, and they wouldn't be able to see what was going on, so he could sing this song in there over the phone.

RON ST. GERMAIN

So he's in DC lock-up, and it was kind of a communal effort between the guys in the band and Anthony. Calls were made to set this up where he could call me on a specific day and time, and he would be able to sing this song over the phone to New York. I booked a studio right below Studio 54 called

Soundworks, which was kind of the Steely Dan haunt, and I knew the tech there. The guy in the jail, instead of having him call from a pay phone, actually let him call in from the guy's office, 'cause the guy thought it was pretty cool that H.R. was going to sing over the phone and he left him alone in there.

H.R.

I picked up the phone and called the operator and asked if I could make a collect call. Thank goodness somebody was there on the other end to receive it. Ron was there, picked up the call and began to play the music back, and they asked me if I would, to the best of my ability, give them some vocals, and that's what I did over the phone. They recorded it and put it down on that record.

RON ST. GERMAIN

The real kicker is, H.R. always traveled with his Bible. They actually let him have it in jail. Those first couple of pages were real thin, kind of onion skin. He had always cleaned his herb on the first page on the Bible 'cause it wouldn't mess up anything. Just before we recorded, I could hear he was smoking something. I said, "What are you doing, man?" He says, "I'm sparking one." I said, "Huh?" He said, "Yeah, you remember the page in the Bible?" He actually ripped that page out the Bible, rolled it up and sparked it. There was so much resin on the page, he actually got a buzz. He's in the slammer for pot, and he's inside smoking his Bible.

He also finished the lyrics to the song in there. The experience of him being in there I think directly relates to it: "I'm in here, you're out there, don't take our business out on the street." It made him actually complete the song. There is a tape of that whole thing somewhere because I had a room mic in the control room and there was one out in the studio. It's there somewhere, but I've never been able to find it. It's a shame because it's a real piece of musical history. It's a great story. At the time we talked to Letterman and a couple of other shows, and they didn't even believe us. They didn't even want to listen to the tape. I suppose if it was Bruce Springsteen, they would have listened.

In all my travels around the world, even though that record never even went gold, anywhere I go on the planet, people come up to me, "Oh, my God, *I Against I* changed my life." There is no record that I have done in forty-plus years that gets that kind of reaction. Once in a while, Aretha Franklin, Whitney Houston, whoever, but nothing that gets that kind of passion. You know, there's one Mick Jagger, there's one Bob Dylan, and there's only one H.R. Why do some bands explode and become the Led Zeppelins of the world and others don't? He had that potential, but it's a lot of other things that need to happen besides just having the talent and ability.

MARK ANDERSEN

At this point, things start spinning out of control. For anybody who's followed Joseph's career, you would see him play with Human Rights and you'd be impressed, and then you'd hear about crazy stuff that was going on. Human Rights wasn't really going anywhere in particular. It was doing okay, but at a certain point, you gotta break through or you can't make it. You've got to calibrate what your expenses are with what you're bringing in, or your enterprise is failing. Human Rights was supposed to play in New York, and the folks at the club are waiting. It's late. Joseph walks in, and they're like, "Cool, you're here." They were scared he wasn't going to show. "Where's the rest of the band?" they ask. There is no band. He hands the guy a cassette and says, "Play this, and I'll sing along with it." "I'm sorry. That doesn't cut it." These kinds of stories start building up about Joseph. He's essentially homeless and going from place to place. In one situation, he barricaded himself inside the apartment of one of his friends from the Madam's Organ days and refused to leave. They let him be for several days because he needed a place to stay. But the time had come to move out, so that the other guy could move in—the guy who's actually paying the rent. Joseph wouldn't do it. He punched out one of the housemates. These kinds of incidents start piling up, and there is a cloud around him. He's acting out in other ways, too, and it comes to a head with his one-time friend, Jimi Riley, who was part of the Olive Tree crew living at the 17th and U house. Jimmy was gay, and he was coming out. He decided to do an interview with H.R. for the *WDC Period*, giving him a chance to respond to the rumors that were swirling around him. In this interview, H.R. spouts more antigay rhetoric and also says, "If a woman is inconsistent in her obedience, it is the responsibility of her man to set her right." It's just terribly disheartening.

9. WITH THE QUICKNESS 1987–1990

I had moved toward Jah, but I wished I could have gotten better professional advice about the situation, and taken a more responsible and professional approach to what was going on in my life, and in my career at that time.
-H.R.

ANTHONY COUNTEY

We're doing some gigs around the time of *I Against I* around 1987, and Chris Blackwell wanted to sign the band to Island Records. There may have even been a discussion with Chris about H.R. portraying Bob Marley in a movie as well, but I'm not a hundred percent sure.

EARL HUDSON

I think there was a bidding war going around, trying to get the Brains signed, and I even heard that Chris Blackwell wanted H.R. to play Bob in a movie, but it never came

ROCK HOTEL & THE NEW MUSIC SEMINAR PRESENT

BAD BRAINS
CIRCLE JERKS

VERNON REID'S LIVING COLOUR

MON. JULY 13
16 and over with i.d./21 to drink

LEEWAY

Doors 7pm
Show starts at 8

10·18

TICKETS: $12 ADV.
$13 DAY.

515 WEST 18TH ST. (at 10th Ave.) 212/645-5157

Tickets at TICKETMASTER. 212/307-7171

PRODUCED BY CHRIS WILLIAMSON AND JOHN SCHER

to be. I think Island and Chrysalis wanted to sign us, and Joe didn't want to sign. It had a lot to do with the management, too. 'Cause the manager dude was kind of, you know, we love him, but dude is still kinda shady from our perspective and not being up front about a lot of things and not accounting for a lot of things. That's why it's always hard for us to try and get back together and have him be the manager.

ANTHONY COUNTEY

We played a show at 1018, which was the old Roxy roller rink. It was the big show for the New Music Seminar that year in 1987. 1018 had 3,500–4,000 people there. It was packed. They played a great set and Chris was there to meet the band. We weren't going to get anything done there necessarily, but it would have been good to at least have gotten to introduce H.R. to Chris Blackwell. H.R. was like, "I've got to go to the bathroom." It was right after the show and the place was emptying out, so there were crowds going out of this big club. He walked right out the door. He was gone—just gone. We were going to open up for U2. They had just released *The Joshua Tree*, and that was on Island, so it was going to be the U2 Joshua Tree Tour with Bad Brains. The record would have been *Quickness*, I guess, but it didn't happen. H.R. wouldn't sign. He didn't trust Chris Blackwell at all.

EARL HUDSON

It could have been a big band at that time. We was trying to see if Gary and Darryl wanted to do some reggae stuff and they didn't want to do it. They wanted to stick primarily to rock, and that's where the next tussle came around.

ILL BILL

I was way into his H.R. solo stuff. *Singin' in the Heart* was a dope album. Human Rights . . . he killed it, and the musicians he was working with were top-notch. There were joints that I feel, if they were marketed and pushed on a pop level, he could have had that Eddy Grant, "Electric Avenue" kind of hit.

KENNY DREAD

After that first album, H.R. had gone back to Bad Brains for a couple of years. When he left them again around 1987, we had some lineup shuffles, and another H.R. album came out, which was the Human Rights album on SST. There was sort of a pool of musicians that moved in and out of the group, kind of swapping and switching for various tours and albums. There was also Zion Train.

JULIE BIRD

Zion Train is the passage to paradise and might just be a shift of consciousness, if you will. It was a roots, rock, reggae band, and a lot of the players in Zion Train joined H.R. on other recordings. Ras Michael was always a teacher. He felt the *Nyabinghi*,[7] and the soulful, spiritual songs that they used to go down to the river and sing. Ras Michael is like a prophet for many people. He remembers the history, and he could bring the old into the new.

H.R.

He was introduced to me through Kenny Dread, and he said he'd be interested in playing some songs together, doing some recordings and playing some live performances. It was a spiritual and educational experience. I learned a lot from him, and I am still learning a lot from him til this day.

---

[7]*Nyabinghi: ritual drumming that's part of a communal meditative practice among Rastafarians*

AL "JUDAH" WALKER

We went to Jamaica to record the Zion Train album at Dynamic Studios in Kingston, which is right around the corner from Bob Marley's studio, Tuff Gong. We stayed in Ocho Rios in a huge place that used to be a skating rink, so we had plenty of space to rehearse. We recorded all the tracks in one night and Joe took the tracks to Ras Michael for him to put his vocals on the songs.

RAS MICHAEL

Yes, that album was a mystical album. We did it through love for Joseph. We did live shows either once or twice. Him open for me [with Human Rights], and then me come on and play, but H.R. want me to play with him, too. Me and H.R. go to Europe, too. Through the most high, H.R. flow with love.

KENNY DREAD

It was our 1989 tour of Europe. This was a pretty low-key tour—all reggae, not a rock tour, and he still did a standing backflip during every show throughout Europe. Every gig. It was unbelievable.

RON ST. GERMAIN

After *I Against I*, I worked on the *Quickness* album for Caroline Records, which was a great record, but H.R. was gone. I worked on that with a couple of other vocalists and also mixed a live record called *The Youth Are Getting Restless.* H.R. kept being like, "I'm going solo." I said, "What do you mean you're going solo? Your record just came out. You're not Mick Jagger. You haven't been in the Rolling Stones for twenty years and had all these amazing hits and played all around the world. Work *this* thing. You gotta work this thing for a while, 'cause you're just becoming known." He says, "Yeah, I'm going solo. I've got to sing for my people." It's always a struggle. You struggle with him because of who he is. We tried like eight songs with this guy Chuck Mosley first and then Taj Singleton. At that point, I went to the label and I said, "Listen, I've got some blazing tracks here. I tried it with this guy, I tried it with this other guy. We don't have a singer."

CHUCK TREECE

At the time, I was in a hardcore group out of New York called Underdog that was on Caroline Records, and Bad Brains, at the time, was on Caroline, too, about to release *Quickness*. There was a lot of controversy about whether H.R. was going to be involved in it and how long he'd be around. They started writing again with Mackie Jayson from the Cro-Mags as the drummer, and they decided they wanted to do something different. So they got Taj Singleton to sing, but Taj wasn't aggressive enough and didn't work out. Darryl and Mackie came to see me play with Underdog in New York, and they approached me and said, "We're looking for a lead singer. Would you mind auditioning?" So I went to Woodstock, and I started hearing the *Quickness* instrumentals. They wouldn't play me anything Taj did. They were like, "You're gonna have to sit in this room with kids running around like crazy," all of them jumping off the steps, and I'm there with a four-track and microphones and monitors. Doc's like, "You have to write all this music here in my house. You don't get a room to go into and close the door." I had to become a family member before I knew if I was ever going to be in the group. You're trying to write like one of your heroes in the guitar player's house, and there are kids running around 'cause that's what kids want to do. I'm just self-absorbed and want to go into a hole, but it made me realize that you can't judge any situation when you're asked to do something intense. And that was an intense chore for me, to audition for the Bad Brains. I wrote like four or five songs and rehearsed with them once, but they wanted H.R. and I can't compare to H.R.

RON ST. GERMAIN

I said, "If you can't find a singer, maybe we can get H.R. back. Maybe we just have to wait until H.R. can come back, but I can't waste any more time with this." It was at that point that we started planning how to get H.R. into the studio. There were a lot of phone calls to his mom. I said to H.R., "I'll come down and get you, man." I got him and we went into RPM Studios on 12th Street in the Village. I had instrumental mixes that I gave him, and he did the whole thing in, I think, one or two days. He just whacked it out. I had what lyrics he had written out, and we'd change and add and write on the fly, and that's how we did that one. The vocals really brought that album together. It's one of my favorite records.

EARL HUDSON

Without H.R., there is no Bad Brains, because we've built a solid rock where the fans only want to see the original band. They're not gonna come to the show if we go out there fake, calling it the Bad Brains. God doesn't want it to happen like that because this is H's band. The Bad Brains is H.R.'s band. Without the lead singer, what the hell? We can call it The Brains or whatever, and have me, Darryl and Gary go out there and play without a lead singer and have one of us try and sing. But what sense does it make to put someone else in there? Look at all the other bands that tried to do that. It doesn't happen.

Quickness featured what turned out to be the most controversial song of the Bad Brains' career, "Don't Blow Bubbles." The album's sixth song, with lyrics composed by H.R., appeared to most to be a rail against homosexuality, although when asked over the years, H.R. claimed it was about everything from a simple warning concerning health consciousness, to a tune about Michael Jackson's pet chimpanzee.

The following excerpt is taken from a discussion that took place between Howie Abrams and H.R. in the spring of 2016:

HOWIE ABRAMS: Was the song "Don't Blow Bubbles" actually about homosexuality?" You've claimed that it was not in the past.

H.R.: Yes, it is. At the time, I wanted people to be aware of certain health risks.

HOWIE ABRAMS: Would you write a song like that today if you had the opportunity to do it again?

H.R. No, I wouldn't. I had no idea how much trouble it would cause. I still consider myself a religious person, and I very much believe in God, but God loves everybody. I feel strongly that we need to live and let live. I really never meant to hurt or upset anyone with the lyrics to that song.

ANTHONY COUNTEY

After we finished the *Quickness* sessions, we went on a tour of America and then we went to Europe. Europe wasn't that many shows, maybe twenty-five to thirty. And after the European tour, he was just done—toast. We did no more touring. They started fighting on the road. H.R. was beginning to be somewhat delusional.

MARK ANDERSEN

They're on tour, driving through East Germany, and a huge fight breaks out. Essentially, from Darryl's point of view, Joseph just flips out suddenly and attacks him—physically attacks him—and they're fist-fighting as they're driving down the road. You know, like, they're driving through East Germany and H.R. is fighting Darryl Jenifer. Finally, they stop the bus. H.R. jumps off and starts walking. To his credit, Darryl got off and walked with him and tried to talk him out of stuff. As fate would have it, the band made it to the show and played their show, but it was clear Bad Brains was coming to an end again. This time, however, Darryl did the single thing that he knew would most affect Joseph: he cut off his dreadlocks. In Rasta circles that's a very powerful symbol. The dreadlocks Darryl had were very long and suddenly they're just gone. It was his rebuke to Joseph. Basically he was saying, "You talk about brotherhood, but you're all about yourself. Fuck your version of Rasta!" It is heartbreaking, and you feel for the guys 'cause these guys have kids now. It's not just hypothetical. They've got to make ends meet or their families will go hungry, and they're depending on Joseph— who can't be depended on.

JIMMY GESTAPO

When you're on fucking tour, man, you're living with the same people twenty-four hours a day, every day for thirty or forty days. People that have nine–to–five jobs like to ask,

"Why do you fight so much with the band?" I was like, "When have you ever lived with anyone in your family or your coworkers twenty-four hours a day, seven days a week, for a month at a time without a break?" You go to work every day, and you get to go home. You're on fucking tour, you are in a vehicle, you're in a club, you're in some shitty little hotel with everybody farting, and everyone's fucking problems pop out. People bug out.

10. LET LUV LEAD (THE WAY) 1990-1994

I'm playing the music I love, so because of that love, it doesn't become a labor, but more like a fulfillment of something you're thirsting for.

-H.R.

EARL HUDSON

H.R. wanted to focus more on just playing reggae music. I think he was done with the aggressive violent punk rock stuff. I think that phase of his life was over. It's something that is a part of us, punk rock music, and then you have reggae music, too. That's why we always tried to blend that stuff. It depends what you want to do in life. If you don't want to do it no more, you don't have to do it. We're not seventy or eighty years old, so we are still healthy enough to play rock music, so I don't think there would be a problem doing that, but he's the lead singer, and if he doesn't want to do that, then we can't really do that anymore. If he wants

to play reggae and if everybody in the band wants to back him doing that, then so be it, but if not, go do what you want to do. Go do your own thing.

ENGLISHMAN | HUMAN RIGHTS

We got into the studio and did the *Charge* album after H.R. quit Bad Brains again, when they were touring after *Quickness* came out. It was a real nice vibe—positives vibes. H.R. just came in and sang a melody, or he'd bang it out on the piano. Me and Earl would rub it down a l'il bit. Then he'd say, "That's it. Yes, Rasta, that's it." We just went from track to track nonstop like that. You can see when you listen to *Charge*, it's free-flowing.

NICK HEXUM

Charge: that's just packed with great songs and great reggae performances. I thought it was amazing, rootsy reggae. We had the album in heavy, heavy rotation when we were making our 311 debut; that was definitely a big influence, and I think the H.R. influence had a lot to do with that.

CHINO MORENO

When I heard the *Charge* record and when I saw him on that tour, I was blown away. It was him lost in the music, and every word coming out of his mouth, every feeling, was completely honest. You could just tell that's what he wanted to do and that's where his heart was. I was probably more blown away by that album than the Bad Brains' *Quickness*. It was almost like another Bad Brains record, even though it wasn't hardcore in any way. It had that same passion that *Quickness* had for me, and if I am correct, it came out shortly after *Quickness*, so it was like another Brains record, full of passion and great songs, and his voice, and his melodies—everything was tip-top.

H.R.

I wound up moving into a neighborhood not too far from Maggie Walker Elementary School in Richmond, Virginia. There were original buildings there built by slaves during the 1800s. The neighborhood was slightly underdeveloped and not around anybody who liked our kind of music. I'd wake up penniless and not knowing where I was going to get some food to eat. There was a horrible, horrible winter storm and I called up my friend Larry Dread. He was a young kid from Korea. He had often asked me if I wanted to come to California, and in the event that I did, he would be able to provide the money for a plane ticket. There was about two to three feet of snow everywhere, so I called him up on the phone and said, "Please help get me out of here," and he said, "Okay, everything cool Rasta, everything cool." Eventually he came up with the money. For me it was an incredible dream come true. I hopped on that plane so fast and flew my sweet little self out to California.

ALLAN AGUIRRE | SCATERD FEW

In 1990, Joseph called me and said that he was coming to the West Coast without his band to do a series of shows in support of *Charge* and asked if my band would be the backup band. I was honored by that request. He could have called pretty much anyone. This is right after *Quickness*. Bad Brains were doing really well, and *Charge* is an excellent album, so I spent the next three to four weeks whipping my boys into shape and learning it. If you can replicate your album live, I always think that's gonna make for a better show, so it was my goal that we replicate *Charge*. Scaterd Few consisted of my brother, Omar, on bass; Samuel on drums; Jamie Mitchell on electric guitar; I was the vocalist; and my brother on keyboards. We flushed out the whole album, then went straight into the studio and started rehearsing with H.R. He might have been surprised at how easy it was. He just needed to sing. Then we jumped in the

van and went up and down the West Coast. We did about a
month's worth of shows. H.R. did a radio interview in San
Francisco, where he said something like, "I'm doing this
now. I'm not really focusing on the Bad Brains." He basically
hands off the mantle of Bad Brains to Scaterd Few. It was
quite the compliment.

LARRY DREAD | FRIEND, MUSICIAN

H.R. came up with the *Rock of Enoch* songs so we started
recording that with him and the band Scaterd Few. Then we
were traveling up and down, spreading Jah love. Spreading
the music of universal peace, love and unity. What the bible
teaches us: Love God, love your neighbors.

ALLAN AGUIRRE

He wrote *Rock of Enoch* in our backyard when he stayed with
us in Burbank. We went to this studio—I think it was called
The Kitchen Sink in Los Angeles—and Scaterd Few did all the
music for it. His wife, or common-law girlfriend at the time, was
named Mary—a wonderful, beautiful woman, very elegant. If
you think of a Nubian queen, she represented this whole deal.
A very nice lady. We really liked her. She came out probably a
month after he was at our house. We said, "Yeah, sure, you can
bring her out," and they had a little girl named Shashamane.
So Mary and the baby came out, and they stayed with us for
close to a month. I was watching H.R. play the role of father
and husband. Very sweet to her, very kind. It was interesting
to see that side of it. He asked me once a long time ago, "How
do you do it? How do you stay married to your wife?" I said,
"You accept the fact that this is the only human being on the
planet that you're gonna take crap from, and you're gonna
submit and let them do that. I have a covenant relationship
with this woman and would do anything to keep it going." I'm
watching his family dynamic, and he's watching mine, 'cause
I have a four-year-old kid and a two-year-old. Anyway, *Rock of
Enoch* gets recorded, and he leaves.

JAMEKEE | D.I.A. RECORDS

When Skitch, Englishman, Al Anderson, Randy Choice and Earl Hudson were backing H.R. as Human Rights, those were his best players, and no one else came close, with the exception of Doc, Darryl and Earl as Bad Brains.

AL ANDERSON

That band was really heavy. Skitchy was the lead guitarist at that time, and I was playing rhythm. We started a tour in Detroit. I was on Skitchy's side, and I was asking him where the chords were going, where the verses were, and he was hipping me on how to play the music. So for the first couple weeks, I just sat in and played rhythm guitar and let him do his thing. Skitchy's amazing. Him and Dave Byers were the scariest guys in the world. When I had to play in the same place as Dave Byers, I was scared, man. This guy had the gnarliest guitar sound I ever heard. He would descend and ascend and not stop grinding. He'd always land on his feet.

RANDY CHOICE | H.R. BAND

We were playing at the Bayou here in Washington, DC, and there's a break in the song where everything stops, and at that break, Joe did a backflip and one of his dreads hits Earl's cymbal right on the downbeat. It wasn't just a performance for performance sake; it all meant something. The movements, the interaction with the audience; it was a lyric in and of itself.

AL ANDERSON

He probably had the strongest pipes I've ever heard, and he could hold a note longer than anybody. He had that circular breathing down. He was doing this while holding notes, and harmonizing. Nobody has the strength he has. I mean, Ronnie James Dio had that power, but H has a falsetto nobody has. He has the ability to throw it and bring it back like few singers I have performed with. The amazing thing is that he could go on for hours, and keep his voice at a decibel that for me was above normal.

Poor Davey Byers passed. I heard before he passed away that he gave up guitar playing, but these are the guys who pretty much introduced me to how to play with H.R. Skitchy was an outstanding lead guitarist, and unfortunately he's passed as well—got into a bad car crash. We had all these bad things going against us. We overworked. We did two sets a night sometimes and had to drive like five hundred miles in between shows, so it was wearing on all the guys in the band. We did it for two years straight, and then H.R. went back to Bad Brains. They couldn't find anyone who could replace him. How could they?

ERIC WILSON | SUBLIME, LONG BEACH DUB ALLSTARS

It was probably like '92, and H.R. wound up staying at my pad for a couple of days. He's a trip to hang out with, that's for sure.

RAS MG/MARSHALL GOODMAN | SUBLIME, LONG BEACH
                                                    DUB ALLSTARS

Sublime ended up playing a show with H.R. at Bogart's in Long Beach. We were the opening act. It was myself, Eric and Brad at the time. Miguel was onstage as well during that period. I guess a lot of reggae artists sometimes used bands to back them up, especially the solo singers, and that's what H.R. did. We played as Sublime, and then played with H.R. too. We already knew all the Bad Brains songs because we are huge fans. And then we did a lot of his Human Rights stuff: "Rasta" and "Shame in Dem Game."

MIGUEL HAPPOLDT | SUBLIME, LONG BEACH DUB
ALLSTARS, SKUNK RECORDS

We knew the promoter, Steve Zepeda and he says "It's H.R. without the Bad Brains. He's doing his solo reggae thing." We were like, that's cool. We were really excited about it. We were already making flyers and then he calls me and says, "Hey, we have bad news. We are canceling that show with H.R. He can make it, but his band can't. He wanted to come anyway and read poetry or something like that, but I don't think it will sell tickets." We had been so fired up to do it. I was like, "Wait, *he* can make it but his band can't?" I go, "Actually that's kind of good. We know a lot of the songs. We play a lot of those songs in our set right now. We could probably back him." So he asked H.R. if he was interested in that.

ERIC WILSON

Sublime had a big library of covers we liked playing at parties. We'd play "House of Suffering," "I Against I," "I Luv I Jah," and a bunch of others. The owner of Bogart's let us practice at the club two days before the show. H.R. showed up there, and we were just kids at Disneyland. I ran up to H.R. with Brad telling him, "We play this, and we can we play that." I remember I asked him if we could play "House of Suffering," and he told me I could have it. He said, "It's yours, man. You can have it," like, I can now own the Bad Brains song "House of Suffering."

ALLAN AGUIRRE

Next thing I know, Bad Brains are recording an album without H.R.

MARK ANDERSEN

In the early 1990s, punk rock was going through the roof. The stuff which was the ugly noise of the misfit, the fuck-up and the loser is the new rock mainstream. "Smells Like

Teen Spirit" tore the roof off the punk underground, and if you look at that video, there are only two band T-shirts that you notice there: Dave Grohl is wearing a Scream shirt, and repeatedly, you see a person wearing a Bad Brains shirt. It's clearly meant to be there, to be a tip of the hat to one of the real pioneers, one of the true trailblazers. But that band doesn't exist anymore. Gary was bringing different singers in, some of them really embarrassing. You're trying to step into H.R.'s shoes, and you can't do it. No one could. They got Israel Joseph I, and he was much better, but still, it's just not Bad Brains.

ISRAEL JOSEPH I | BAD BRAINS VOCALIST ON *RISE*

They were holding auditions in New York, and I was doing my reggae in the City with our band, Uprising. We backed up Eek-A-Mouse. We backed up one of the Marley kids when he was really young. We backed up a whole lot of people as a reggae band. I was sound asleep at a point where there were no cellphones and hardly any beepers or pagers. I'm at my mom's crib sleeping, and I get a knock on my bedroom door, and she says, "It's the telephone." I grab the phone and say,

"Hello?" This deep rich dark tone came on and said, "Is this Israel? This is Darryl Jenifer of the Bad Brains." I said, "Come on, man. Who is this?" The voice was calm and he laughed and said, "Man, this is really Darryl Jenifer." We began talking, and the conversation lasted an hour. He said, "I got your number from Latasha, and she said that you were a singer." He asked if I knew their music and told me they were looking for a singer. He said, "We would like you to come up to Woodstock to try out." We began talking about family. That was the majority of the conversation, about family, and what family is about and what life is about, and at the end of the conversation, he said, "All right, cool. We're going to have you come up." He sent me a Greyhound ticket, and I got on the bus. So I'm there, and we lit up a spliff. It was dark, and the TV was on. We sat there and smoked and just talked. The next morning, we got up and we were going to rehearse. They asked me if I knew "Re-Ignition," and I said, "Of course." So we do "Re-ignition," and it is banging. I mean, it sounds like the record. I start singing the vocals, and because I love this song so much and love H.R.'s voice, and because Jah Rastafari was meaning for something to happen, I sang like the record. After the first verse, Darryl stopped playing. He said, "Hold up on the mic, hold up. That sounds just like H.R." Doc turned around and started messing with his guitar, and he said, "Youth, you sound just like Joe." He told me he was closing his eyes and thought it was Joseph singing. I told them, "These are Joe's songs, so I'm not going to sing them like me. I'm going to sing them like him. I want to pay homage to the Rastaman." He asked me if I could write rock songs, and we played a few more songs. Darryl eventually came over to me, and he said, "Do you want to be down with this?" I said, "What do you mean, be in the band?" He said, "Yeah."

CHUCK TREECE

At that time, I had started playing drums in the band. We found Israel through this girl in New York and he was great, so we started going through all the motions of getting songs together. We had about four or five songs, and they started talking to Ron St. Germain, and Ron thought that having Mackie on the record would be stronger because Mackie had played with the band longer and he felt like Mackie was a better drummer. It's a blow to the ego, but those things happen. They were signed to Epic Records through Living Colour, because they were going to be touring with Living Colour. They did the tour, and that's when I joined the band. It was kind of a whole new Bad Brains, and Beau Hill ended up producing the record. There was a twisted vibe about that whole situation.

ANTHONY COUNTEY

Well, it was kind of good. It was a decent year and a half. It was a real band with a real record. Everybody got along pretty well. They toured and toured and toured. It was sort of Bad Brains the way it was supposed to be. It wasn't H.R., though. Israel is Israel.

H.R.

I didn't feel betrayed when they brought in another singer. I didn't respond as if it was betrayal, but more like a stepping stone that paved the way for the authentic group to eventually reform. When one door closes, another door opens.

11. VOYAGE INTO INFINITY 1994–1995

You can't make everybody happy, but if you try sometimes, you get what you need. Don't look back; keep moving forward. That's what I did. I kept on moving forward.

-H.R.

H.R.

We've had many transformations. We've gone through about seventeen or eighteen different generations, and I keep meeting youngsters who want to climb on board—asking me if there is room for me to try them out. I'd say, "We'll see, we'll see." I met some youngsters in California, The Crabiteers: Al and Jamie, and his brother Andy. They were inspiring after another break from the Brains.

ANDY RONDON | THE CRABITEERS

At that time, he was really on top of his game. A stickler for music academia. We lived together for a long time, and it was a growing time for us as players and musicians. When you worked with Joe, it was a school's-in-session kind of thing. And H.R. truly knew everyone, from the rich and famous to the completely unknown. He loved surfing. He loved the water; Spent a lot of time at the beach in North San Diego County where he had some friends. He'd just kind of bounce back-and-forth. He would never really spend too much time with anyone in particular, and he never had a problem picking up a bag and moving around a lot.

JAMIE MITCHELL | THE CRABITEERS

Andy and H.R. were living together in our rehearsal studio. It was getting a little tense, and H.R. needed to move out. So Andy said to me, "You've got that apartment and everything," so I picked Joseph up and he moved in. We were like two peas in a pod. It was like my stepdad came to town. I was going to junior college, and we were doing shows on the weekends. I would wake up in the morning and he would be like, "Gotta get your breakfast, son." And he would make me potatoes with soybean powder and some milk with spirulina sprinkled on top of it. That was followed by a massive cone of weed. He'd be like, "You ready for school, son?" I'd walk the five blocks to school, just out of my mind high, but my life was really happy. It was cozy with Joe there. However, there were a few things that happened that just made me uncomfortable.

Here I was with one of my musical heroes; we sold out three nights at the Dragonfly, and we played at Long Beach Arena with General Public as our opening act, and Eek-A-Mouse playing after us. I was kind of living my dream, but there were parts of the dream that were not necessarily dreamy. It saddens me to have this memory. I realize now what happened with Joseph. The manager from my building—I'm not gonna say everything that happened—but he observed behaviors that were happening when I was gone at school

or at my girlfriend's place. This happened outside of our apartment. I just should have been there. I should have been there to take care of my bro but I wasn't old enough to process what was happening to him. He wasn't trying to fuck with me or mess with anybody; he was just dealing with his own self. So I would be gone and things would happen at the apartment, and I would come home and Joseph would be a really different person. When you're with somebody all the time, and you love them and make intense art with them, and you're at the peak of what you're doing with this person . . . when you have that down time together, it can be awkward. And when you add the element of someone who potentially has some sort of schizoaffective disorder, it festers and can get really crazy. And it got really crazy at the apartment. It got really crazy. If I'm totally honest about it, I abandoned the apartment, and I abandoned Joe there. Things were getting so strange, I had to leave.

ANDY RONDON

There were times when the guy was just gone. Totally and absolutely gone. We would be backstage ready to perform, and he would literally go through these psychoses of hearing people, and turning the lights off and telling everybody to be quiet. And we're sitting there just praying to the good Lord Almighty: *I just want to go home. I just want to make it home and make it through this night.*

EARL HUDSON

He was kinda struggling living out there in California. I don't know what the hell he was doing out there. He was trying to do music, too, but . . . I don't know, man . . . he was tripping. He was going through some things.

MARK ANDERSEN

So after nearly two decades of ups and downs, Bad Brains are finally offered that big deal, that major-label deal that has been out there for a decade, the one that H.R. had walked away from numerous times. Madonna's label, Maverick Records, wants the Bad Brains, and Joseph signs on the dotted line. The original Bad Brains, back in the studio with Ric Ocasek to record their new record *God of Love*. It's like the stars have aligned. We haven't seen Bad Brains since *Quickness*. They deserve a shot like this. They were out there, blood, sweat and tears on the punk rock trail, blazing that trail for everybody—including Nirvana.

CHINO MORENO

We had just gotten signed to Maverick Records in '95, and one of the first conversations I remember having with Guy Oseary was him asking me what my biggest influences were. I said, "Today I'm listening mostly to Sade and the Bad Brains; those are my favorite two artists I listen to most throughout the day. That's what I like." It was probably a few weeks after that he gave me a call and said he ran into H.R. and he invited me and H.R. over to his house. H.R. took us to some Ethiopian restaurant. We had dinner and went back to Guy's house. Me and H.R. sat in a little room and played some music together. He had his trumpet with him and I had a guitar. We sat in this spare room and just jammed. I was twenty years old at the time and hanging out with one of my biggest influences.

EARL HUDSON

Darryl and Gary were in New York and were pissed off at the drummer dude they had, so they wanted me to go to Australia. I went with them. They used this other cat to sing, but it turned out that the cat wasn't good and people wanted to see H. H.R. was in California and met Madonna's A&R cat, and dude asked what it would take to get the Bad Brains to record again. So that's when we pulled H back in and did the album *God of Love*. We got the Bad Brains back on track for a little bit longer, and that, you know, didn't last.

GUY OSEARY | MAVERICK RECORDS

I was backstage at Lollapalooza and H.R. was there. I walked up to him and I introduced myself, and he said, "Oh, let me have your number." I gave him my number and saw that on one side of the paper he gave me, it said "Adam Yauch" with his number. And I thought, *Oh, they're probably trying to sign the Bad Brains, too*. Once I saw Adam Yauch's name on the back of the paper, I thought, *Okay, Grand Royal's gonna try and beat me to the punch*, so I immediately got on it.

CHINO MORENO

A couple of days after that, Guy was like, "I want to sign them, I want to get them a deal." I was like, "You need to do this. They are one of the best bands ever." More than anything, I wanted to hear a new Bad Brains record. *God of*

Love was made, and when they went on tour, we were the band they took with them. I think it lasted six shows.

ANTHONY COUNTEY

Guy checked in with me and said he wanted to do something with the band, and wanted to know what I thought. I told him the truth. I told him it's extremely unpredictable, and he shouldn't expect much—although from my point of view, it will always be worth trying. The band wanted to try, but it gets very complicated. Gary Gersh wanted to sign them as well, but he didn't call me. There was a certain point when Adam wanted to bring them out to LA to meet labels and stuff. I was, like, "Sure, that's cool, but don't you need me there?" They basically didn't want me there, which was cool with me because it's how they wanted it. So they went and had a meeting with Gary Gersh, and at the same time Guy and Freddy DeMann from Maverick are on the phone with me, saying the whole time, "We really want to do this, Anthony." I said, "Well, we'll see how it comes out." I think H.R. was just waiting for Gersh to call me, but he wouldn't tell him that, so when they didn't, H.R just got up from that meeting and went over to Maverick. The deal was done the same day. It was crazy. Such a funny situation. I think Gary was smart not to have signed them. We did get the record out, and to me that is an important thing.

EARL HUDSON

He was acting weird, but he signed the contract. We rented a house in Beverly Hills and recorded out in California. We all signed the contract at the dinner table.

DEB JONES | MANAGEMENT ASSISTANT

We rented a house for two to three months and H.R., I guess, wanted to bring me into the family. He wanted to make sure I was aware of Bad Brains—what they stood for and what he stood for. He made sure I read the bible, made sure that I knew about Rastafari and made sure I was schooled in their camp before I could start working with them. H.R. had a whole suite to himself. He had his own bathroom and everything. It was California and it was very hot, and I remember him having the temperature up to the max. He had a separate thermostat up there, and it would be so hot. I would go visit him and he would sit me down, literally crossed-legged in his suite, and he would give me the bible and I would have to read through it whether I understood it or not. I had to repeat certain phrases or certain passages of the bible so that he was satisfied that I knew something about what was going on with him and his beliefs.

AL ANDERSON

He was very much into his Rastafarianism. I really think his faith had a lot to do with his courage to continue to do music, 'cause it seemed to be a time when he wasn't really interested in music anymore, but he went into the spiritual world. Now he's back.

GUY OSEARY

Everything was going pretty good. There were moments making the album where I started to see a glimpse of H.R.'s other side. It was quite concerning, as he'd go in and out of this other side. The first time you see it, you could just chalk it up to, *I don't know, that was weird.* And maybe the second time, *Wow, that's really weird.* And the third time, *Whoa, is this guy clinically ill?* Sometimes it was humorous, so you don't quite know: is this playful, or is there a serious problem here? It became quite obvious later on that there were some serious issues. I remember when the recording was going on and he was having a really bad time. People tried to shelter me from knowing that side, but it was hard to shelter. There was a moment while making the record where he kind of lost his mind.

MARK ANDERSEN

The record comes out, and the music is great, but it's like H.R. isn't there with a couple of exceptions. The lyrics just don't make sense. It doesn't work. And then they came back to DC for a free show down here. A wonderful gesture, and it should have been a triumph, but it's like Joseph doesn't want to be onstage. He's hidden back behind his sunglasses; he's impenetrable. He's cut himself off. He kinda wanders onstage, wanders offstage in the middle of songs. He's kind of singing the lyrics but he's got this crazy grin on his face. I was there in the front row. This wasn't Bad Brains.

AL "JUDAH" WALKER

I went to the show at Trax in Southwest DC around '95 and I couldn't get in because the line was wrapped around the whole club. I already knew that the amount of people outside was the same amount as inside, so I didn't even try to get in there. About twenty minutes later, I saw Joe come out of the side door. We greeted and he said, "Come, let's go on the tour bus." And once we got on the bus, I don't know . . . there was something very different about him.

JUAN DECOSTA

These guys are getting ready to be rock stars, for real. This shit is getting ready to happen, then this muthafucka, as usual, H.R. fucks it up some kind of way. He's just that dark cloud. You're having this perfect day, and all of a sudden, here comes the dark cloud who screws up everything. There are so many different layers to what was happening. He'd turned to Rasta and didn't want to do the punk anymore. I knew there were some struggles in the band with that. This is your brand; this is what you are famous for. You don't want to do this anymore, but this is what the people want. I love Rasta. I love the music. I love the vibe, but if I go see Bad Brains, you're gonna *Pay to Cum* baby!

JOSE GONZALES

Sometimes it seems like he's playing a joke on everybody and amusing himself by being zany or by not paying attention or standing still. Originally, it was my belief that he just didn't want to participate in punk rock music anymore, but it went beyond that. I think he was very tired of being what they wanted him to be. He did a complete turnaround and said, *I'm not going to be that super maniacal front man anymore. I'm just gonna stand here and deliver my message, but not the way you want me to deliver it. I want to deliver it the way I want to deliver it.*

JOHN STABB

The Bad Brains are doing songs that they are full-on into, and he doesn't have any enthusiasm about it. It's obvious onstage that he's just bullshiting his way through the songs. If you still feel it in your heart and you want to do this material, then that's fine and that's cool and everything, but I don't think he wants to be up there unless he's just doing the reggae songs. To me it's a big cop-out. It's like dissing your audience. Why is he bullshitting through the punk stuff, and then he's so into the reggae stuff?

12. SHITFIT 1995

Kids were bouncing off the walls, and the group was playing and it kind of broke out into a riot, I think. I needed a little break, so I spent some time in solitary confinement.

-H.R.

ANTHONY COUNTEY

He was completely unpredictable at this point. I didn't know what was really going on with him. It's not like anything understandable happened. We went on tour with the Beastie Boys in Canada, and he didn't make it onstage for the first show. I really don't know what was going on with him. He just didn't want to go onstage. I don't know why. He had a girl in his dressing room; it was all very strange. He never showed any sign of going onstage. Then he got violent and that was the end of that.

GUY OSEARY

This is the launch of our album, and we couldn't get a better tour. About ten minutes go by before Bad Brains are

supposed to go on at the first show. Fifteen minutes go by. Twenty minutes go by, and Abbey Konowitch and I look at each other and go, "Something's wrong." We start walking out of the arena and I see Mike D from the Beastie Boys, and he's like, "Yo, what's up with your boy?" I didn't know what was going on, but I knew it wasn't good. So I walk up to the tour bus, and H.R. won't come out of the back of the bus. I said, "H.R., you gotta get out here. What's going on here?" And he said, "They're not following correct protocol, and I wasn't asked what the correct protocol was." And I'm not quite sure what he's talking about. He finally comes out of the room, and he literally looks back and takes the back of his hand and smacks Earl. And he's down, his brother is down. Next thing we know, he got into a physical fight with his manager, Anthony. He pulled a whole wad of hair out of his head. He was losing it. The police showed up. I think he had some marijuana on him, so they deported him. Ironically, I was at the airport the next day flying back to LA, and he was on my flight. I didn't say hi. I just saw him sitting there, and I was so angry at him. He didn't see me, but I was so upset . . . they were a beautiful group of guys, musically unbelievable, the Beastie Boys are supporting them, and on your first night, to just not even make it to the stage.

MARK ANDERSEN

Joseph flips out and puts Tony Countey in the hospital. He broke bones in his face, just really dangerous violence. And Tony, to his credit, perhaps because he had nothing but love for Joseph, doesn't press charges. You know, the prophet of love and revolution is beating up one of the best friends he has in the world. Anyone who knows Tony knows how much blood, sweat and tears he's left out on that trail. It shows his love that he didn't press charges.

TERRY ANZALDO | HEAD OF PROMOTIONS, MAVERICK RECORDS

We were getting some airplay on the "God Of Love" single and we were feeling good about everything, and our staff was out there on the road with the band bringing radio to their shows and things of that nature. People were excited. Then we got the call from Guy who witnessed the catastrophe that had happened on the opening night with the Beastie Boys. It was very frustrating. Are we gonna lose the excitement from the outlets that we had set up? Somehow we regrouped; sat down with the band, and put them out on the road with then up-and-coming buzz band, the Deftones.

ANTHONY COUNTEY

H.R. actually came back within days and said he was sorry that all that happened. He wanted to start up again, so we headlined some shows back in the US.

DEB JONES

We were on tour with the Deftones and H.R. didn't make it to one of the shows because he was given the wrong directions to the club. He did not have a flat tire or anything like that. At that time he was traveling with a girlfriend who he insisted be handcuffed to him all the time. I don't know how she put up with it. It was at least ten days or two weeks out on the road that she was along with us. She and H.R. had the back room of the tour bus and they were handcuffed together every time I saw them.

CHINO MORENO

We played a few shows, and the third or fourth show was in San Diego. The night before we were in Los Angeles. H.R. had taken off for the day and went and bought a limousine. He decided he was not gonna ride on the tour bus but instead follow the bus in his limousine. He was gonna drive it. I remember being at the venue—we did soundcheck, and he hadn't shown up yet, so people started saying, "I hope he shows up." We played our set and it was time for the Brains to go on, and he still hadn't shown up. I was talking to Darryl and Doc and they were like, "You wanna come up and do a few songs?" I ended up going up there and doing four or five songs with the band.

GUY OSEARY

H.R. calls me and says, "I'm at a car dealership and I'm going to buy a car, but they need to know that I have someone validating that I have money and can pay for this car. It's a used car. Will you talk to the guy here?" I said, "Okay," and he puts me on the phone with the guy. I said, "I work at the record label, and he's an artist on the label. Can I ask you what kind of car he's getting?" He tells me he's getting a 1978 stretch limo, and I asked him to put H.R. back on the phone. He puts him back on the phone and I go, "H.R., you're buying a limo from 1978?" He goes, "Yeah, it's beautiful." And I said, "Who's gonna drive you?" And he said, "Scotty," who was a guy who worked at our record company that had taken him there 'cause he needed to get a car. So, now he thought Scotty would be his driver. Anyhow, he ended up buying the car. He had that limo and actually took me to lunch in the limo. I sat in the back, and he looked back at me and said, "I hope one day one of my artists can drive me in a limo to lunch."

KEITH MORRIS | CIRCLE JERKS, BLACK FLAG, OFF!

We're backstage at a Beastie Boys show at this outdoor shed space. People want to hang out as bands do, chittin' and chattin' and carrying on, and a couple of hours later, after everybody has cleared out, the people that are putting on the concert, Goldenvoice, said, "People, it's time to go." Everybody's walking out, and I'm with Flea and Anthony Kiedis and a couple of other friends, and we are walking out the doors to the parking lot, and there's H.R. in the stretch limo, driving around. It seemed that he had been driving around the parking lot for at least a couple of hours. Maybe he didn't know where he was at; maybe he didn't care. Maybe it was just something for him to do; maybe, quite possibly, he couldn't find the way out of the parking lot.

ANTHONY COUNTEY

The tour with Deftones moved on to Lawrence, Kansas. Then, it was REALLY over. He clocked a kid in the audience with a mic stand. That brought everything to a grinding halt.

CHINO MORENO

There was a lot of tension at that time with the band, you could see it. At any minute, anything can happen, and that's what happened. I think there were four or five more shows and everything unfolded. Man, I remember H.R. had this girl handcuffed to him for a few days. Every time I saw him get off the bus, she was handcuffed to him. He was in a good mood, smoking and hanging out, but I remember thinking, *This is wild!* Anyway, the show was good. We had a good show, but they only played half a set or something. I was in the crowd watching, and all of a sudden, right in the middle of the set, I saw a mic stand go up and *BOOM!*

A couple of minutes later the cops showed up. I saw them arrest H.R. and take him out. What they were saying was that some dude was spitting on him. The show was over. The tour was over.

H.R.

We were in Lawrence and the group was performing, and everybody in the audience was in pandemonium. I saw a pistol and I took the microphone stand and I went up, and I came down, and I hit the person in the head. I don't know if it was the one who had the gun or what, but I knew I had to get off of that stage. I don't even know to this day if they really did have a gun pointed at Darryl or not, but I didn't want to take any chances. Now we have a lot more organization—better security, bouncers, road crew and technicians—and for that reason, we're not that vulnerable and the kids aren't really a threat to our existence or the sound. At first, I didn't know what to think. I didn't want to stop the music, but the kids were going just wild, jumping up and down, jumping on the stage, jumping all over the equipment, the amplifiers—even me, grabbing my legs, grabbing my pants. I remember them pulling down my pants, and I was trying to vocalize and do my songs and, at the same time, keep my pants on. They put me in protective custody over there in Lawrence.

CHINO MORENO

There had been no bad energy before the show. He was fine. Right before they went on, I smoked with him in the alleyway behind the club and he was happy. He went onstage and he was killing it. It was so out of the blue. Perhaps he did see someone with a gun. Perhaps somebody did spit on him, I don't know. He was singing, and then it was, like, *D'oh!* He kept singing, so he wasn't so frustrated that he couldn't carry on. I remember him walking out in handcuffs and being like, "What's going on?"

ID NO. 36537   DATE 07:21:95

SHERIFF'S DEPARTMENT
LAWRENCE, KANSAS

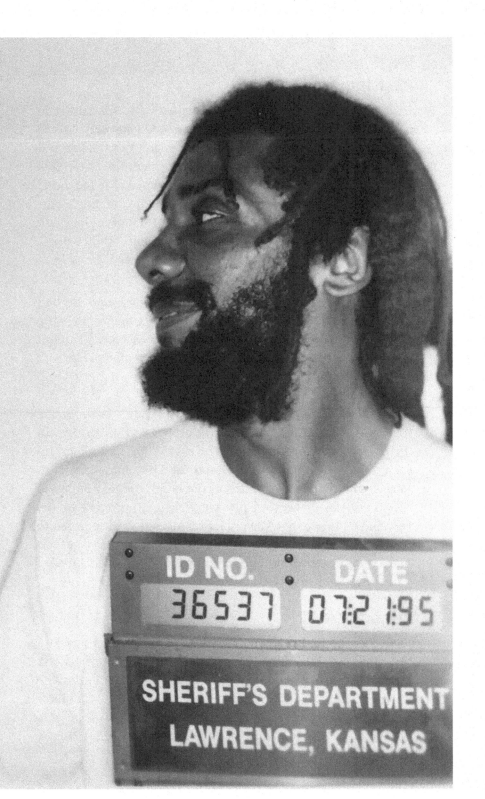

ID NO. DATE

36537 07.21.95

SHERIFF'S DEPARTMENT
LAWRENCE, KANSAS

EARL HUDSON

I think somebody spiked him. Somebody put something in some herb or something. He said this one kid spit on him and he hit the dude over the head with the microphone stand, but I'm back there playing drums, so I didn't see it. He swung that shit like it was a feather, and dude got crowned. The kid didn't press charges, but he still went to jail. Luckily, he didn't hurt the kid too bad. I almost pissed on myself. He was dealing with a lot of stuff. It might be drug-induced, I really couldn't say.

DEB JONES

That particular day we were in a college town and we had a lot of college guys at the show—plus some right wing skinheads, which H.R. absolutely disapproved of. I didn't see any big threatening vibe. I only saw some pockets of skinheads hanging out. They were chanting, "Oi Oi Oi," and having beers. Anthony felt something was in the air and H.R. felt it. What I learned later, and we didn't know at the time, was that H.R. had unfortunately been given certain drugs—mushrooms—and lost the plot. They had blown up their advance for their merchandise. They had blown up tens of thousands of dollars in deals for them because of this madness. It seemed like we were getting right to the very edge. I knew that Maverick was already disappointed to the point where we were screwed if we didn't pull it together. The influences around H.R. were not positive, and I wish I had been more savvy at the time.

GUY OSEARY

That was the end of it for me. I was just like, this guy is a screwup and I couldn't do anything to help him. I don't know how old I was, but I didn't have the education or the experience. I probably still don't, but at that time, I didn't have any experience on how to deal with his psychosis. That was the end of me with H.R. and the end of me with the Bad Brains.

ANTHONY COUNTEY

He did hurt a kid at a show in England once who spit on him. That's what the kids were doing at the shows. It was ridiculous. We tried to stop it from happening, but at some shows, it just would not stop. He perfectly roundhoused a mic right in the side of this kid's head. He cut him right above his eye. If he was off a half-an-inch, he would've killed this kid. He would have hit him in the temple with a very heavy microphone. The same thing happened in Lawrence. H.R. just picked up the microphone stand and hit the kid, swinging it like a baseball bat. There's no point in being angry. H.R. was unpredictable, and I knew that from the beginning. We knew that, especially in 1995. Always hoped that things would get better, that the brotherhood and camaraderie would pay off or work out. You couldn't blame him. His decisions are out of his hands somehow.

You can sit down and get somebody an appointment. They can go to the appointment and they can get nothing done, or they can get something done. It's up to them. He was not interested in recognizing anything or getting anything done about it for a very long time. He could've absolutely had the very best people in the world, psychologists and stuff. Brilliant people who work with people who are really incredibly creative and brilliant like H.R. But the person has to want to do something about their situation.

Creativity is such a secret event or mysterious occurrence. It's not like you can put your finger on it and just know what the fuck is going on. There are things in life that we don't know about, and that's one of the things we live with as intelligent people. We know that we just don't fucking know. Maybe someday we'll know. Who knows?

13. NEW SUN
1995–1998

For me, not having a permanent place to live was a test. I may have been selling out arenas, but at the same time, it was selling me out because I had no place to live.

-H.R.

MARCO ALDACO | FRIEND

I'm driving along Hollywood Boulevard and I see H.R. looking up at the sky and I say, "Oh shit, H.R.'s in town." I wasn't gonna say nothing. He's cool. He's doing his thing, getting some fresh air, getting out and about, checking out the birds. I knew that there had been some issues, and maybe he needed to come inside and hang out for a minute. So I told him, "If you wanna come over sometime and clean up you're more than welcome." I figured I might see him in a week or two, but the very next day, he was there and said, "I'm gonna take you up on your offer."

I didn't really want to ask him too much and get personal, just like, "How you doing? You okay?" Once I got to know him, I started figuring him out as far as when it was good to talk about things, and when it was not good to talk about things, so we basically got to know his little dark side and mood swings. To be in Hollywood that way is not a nice thing. You're on the streets, and there's just way too much stuff to deal with. The fact that maybe some people did recognize him was not really cool; to see a legend that you love going through a situation. On my part, compassion kicked in, and I said, "We've got to do something for H. We can't have this if I can help. I'm gonna help." So we had a little space for him in the office where he could just chill. We made a little bed for him. He didn't really eat much, a lot of vegetables. He was cool most of the time. He learned a little Spanish.

After a while, he said, "Listen, man, I wanna get back with the Brains. Call Earl. Call my brother." I was always getting calls from his mom, Carmen, checking in on him. "How's my son? Make sure he's okay, take care of him." I put him on the phone, and it was nice that he had a place where they could check in on him. We tried to help as much as we could, but he's an adult. We knew there was an issue, and through his belief in Rasta, he would not take any medication. Whenever he was doing good, we did what we could to put a little money in his pocket. One day, we had a little fire. We had an electrical stove, and I never knew that if you turned the stove on just a little bit—it's gonna simmer low. So we were partying in the office, having a good time talking, and I guess somebody must have turned the stove on a bit. We didn't want to say it was H. I get a call about 11:30 from one of the neighbors, who says, "Get over here. Your house is on fire." The fire department was thinking it was an electrical fire caused by this stove we used from the '60s, maybe even the '40s, when this building was built. Again, I didn't want to say it was H. I didn't know who it was. We had heard that he flooded a couple of other apartments. Sometimes things happen. Nothing survived. Everything caught on fire. He pretty much burned the house down. I didn't want to blame it on him or our other roommate, Stuart, 'cause we were all messed up.

ERIC WILSON

He's been homeless since I've known him. When he stayed at my house for a bit, he got a little weird. I didn't like it. He gave my girlfriend a dress. I don't know what he meant by that, if he had a crush on her or what, but I was telling him, "Nah, dude, you can't get on her. That's my girlfriend." One time I was driving down Ocean, and he was walking down the street with a suitcase and a suit on. It looked like he was going to work or something. I didn't want him to see me because I was a little discouraged from last time with my chick and stuff. That was the mother of my kid. I mean, I was around H.R. quite a bit on the road, too, and I've never seen him have any type of aggression or anything. I've seen him talking to himself and stuff, but I haven't seen him have any bad trips.

ANDY RONDON

Totally breaks your heart when you hear about him not doing well, because there were times in his life when he was cruising around, driving a limousine—living in it off and on. That was right around the time Bad Brains did that deal with Maverick Records. They got some dough, and he got a big, extensive wardrobe. I did a show on the Sunset Strip one time with another local band and he showed up dressed as His Royal Highness or something, with a turban and a cape. He was that kind of brother. We would start playing together and do a few shows, and everything would be great. Every show got a little bit nicer and a little bit bigger, and then this pressure came. Professional pressure. And I think at times throughout his career, that's when he would run into walls. It's hard to give you any kind of clinical explanation. There were times backstage before a show where we wouldn't know what was going to happen. We didn't know which Joe we were going to get up onstage. There would be times when he would just be angry at us. Everything would be cool, and it would be packed at the club and everyone is excited. We did shows with Sublime, and then he would do those things. He would refuse to come onstage.

MARCO ALDACO

One day, one of the bookers from House of Blues got a hold of me because they were doing some sort of benefit gig for Bradley Nowell from Sublime. I heard a female voice on the phone—I'm not sure if it was the girl from No Doubt—but she asks if she can speak to H.R. "I want to invite him to a show," she told me. I said, "H, there's someone for you on the phone." He jumps on the plane the next day to come to Los Angeles, and then he's at the Hollywood Palladium onstage. Somehow MTV gets involved where they put out some news from the Palladium.

OPIE ORTIZ | LONG BEACH DUB ALLSTARS

It was a weird time. We were all heavily medicated with alcohol because Brad [Nowell] had just passed, and we were trying to do a benefit show. Brad really looked up to H.R., Eric looked up to him, we all looked up to him as a leader. And for him being there, it just solidified a lot of things for us. When we jammed, it was like, "We have H.R. I don't give a fuck who else is playing. Oh, KRS One is going on after us? Okay, cool." There were times like that which made us as proud as can be to have him there. Whether he was fully one hundred percent or not, he still sang and he still killed it.

MIGUEL HAPPOLDT

We felt blessed to be hanging out with him and that he got on a record with us, but we could tell that he wasn't doing good. The business side wasn't good and his health wasn't that good, but he could still sing perfectly. It was one of those things for us where it was like a family, and we felt bad that he wasn't really living anywhere specific, so we put him up in a hotel. It was like, "Where's he going to go after this?" It was sad, but because we were on this big label, we could give him some cash. I feel like we did a good thing. There was just a lot that we couldn't do. It's one of those things where it's like, "Oh well, if this is the end of our little chapter with Joe, at least it will end on a high note." But it didn't. We went on tour after that, and we did Red Rocks, and we did a bunch of other shows with him. When you spend that kind of time with somebody, you can see the personality shift. A lot of it was how quiet he had gotten. Not like he was ever chatty or anything, but he got really withdrawn.

RAS MG/MARSHALL GOODMAN

When Long Beach Dub Allstars was created, we stayed in touch with everybody that we came across over all the years with Sublime. Barrington Levy, Half-Pint and other people. That's how we got a lot of our guest artists. We'd heard that H.R. was around, and that's how we got the man to do the "New Sun" song, which is phenomenal. We bring H.R. in to write in the studio. With any musician, you never really know what you're going to get, but we had this song together for him. He went and sat behind the piano and had his microphone set up behind the piano and just kind of sat there for a while. So, he was just sitting back there playing the piano as he's singing. If you listen to the solo vocal track, you hear piano tickles and stuff. He did like five vocal takes, because he wanted to dub all these harmonies, and everything started blossoming. When it was done it was just a full vocal extravaganza like I knew he could do. We were lucky enough to get him on that day to do it.

ERIC WILSON

We did a tour with the Dub Allstars, H.R. and Born Jamericans. That was pretty cool. We arranged for him to be on a tour bus together with us, but he wanted to have his own car, so his tour manager rented a car and they followed us across the country. It was a trip.

NOEL BAKER | H.R.'S MANAGER (1998–2004)

While we were doing those dates with Long Beach Dub Allstars, in Colorado, we got to hook up with Darryl Jenifer at Red Rocks. That was the first time H.R. and Darryl had been onstage together in a long time, and that made a mark for the Bad Brains to get back together. It just went from there.

WILLIAM BANKS

He was living on the streets around then and living in different people's homes. He's like a chameleon to me because he adapts to his environment wherever the environment is. H.R.'s living what he's supposed to be living. H.R. is so mystical. You can't put nothing on that man. He got his

road, and he's choosing that road, and he's taking it. Some people choose to live in a house, married, kids, picket fence . . . you choose those lifestyles. That man is nothing but music, and H.R.'s been music all his life.

TOBY MORSE | H2O

What's crazy is he was moving away from punk [with Human Rights]. That's the punkest thing of all: living off the radar, living by your own rules, living how you wanna live and being happy. It's not about money, it's about being happy and doing what you want to do. How is he surviving? Jah's protecting him!

WILLIAM BANKS

Joe used to stand up in a neighborhood where Ras Michael lived, right where guys was selling cocaine on the block. He'd stand there with his arms crossed in the morning and they'd be wondering, *Why is this guy standing there?* Why did H.R. do it? Maybe he was trying to tell them something or give them a message to stop selling it—to stop doing it.

H.R. could go where some people can't even walk down the street without getting harassed. He could walk right there. You begin to understand his mindset.

ISRAEL JOSEPH I

What some men call mental illness today is what people back in the days called "shaman." H.R. is a prophet; a man who leads people spiritually. He is a shaman, and shaman like him and Lee "Scratch" Perry are supposed to be sitting around acting crazy and out of their minds. They are not dealing in this world. He is not supposed to be normal. He is not supposed to be sitting around like, *How are you doing? Welcome to MTV. I'm H.R. and we are going to play a little number for you.* No man! H.R. is and another place. I understand it's hurting his relations with other humans. Look at Jesus: he had disciples around him, and they did not understand the brother, yet they knew something special was going on. This brother has got something to say and is connected in places where we are not connected. Something is happening with this man. He is a little out there, but something's up.

14. SOUL BRAINS
1998–2013

I only wanted to be in a group that was positive and uplifting, so I decided to change the band name and give that a try.
-H.R.

ANTHONY COUNTEY

H.R. called me about them wanting to be called Soul Brains moving forward. I said, "If you want to do Bad Brains, I will do that, but I'm not inventing a new band for a band that already has a name." I asked, "Are you going to write new material?" And he said, "No." "Okay, call it what you want, but if I'm going to do it, I'll do Bad Brains." I didn't do it because it felt too weird, especially changing their name. To come up with a new name was like, *What is this? Whose material are you playing? You're playing the material of a band called Bad Brains?* It was way too confusing for me to be involved like that.

H.R.

I wanted us to have a more positive outlook on life. I didn't want to be into bad anything.

NOEL BAKER

I started off as Joe's road manager with Human Rights. He was getting ripped off by a former manager, and I ended up becoming the manager for H.R. from that point on. H.R. said to me out of the blue, "Let's reunite the Brains and call it the Soul Brains." We had gotten an offer from the San Francisco Maritime Hall for $20,000, so at first we were gonna do a one-off and they decided not to do it. It took me talking to Dr. Know every day for six months to get him to come through. They had a jaded past from what H.R.'s actions had been. They had some history that wasn't as positive as you'd like it to be, and they were a bit apprehensive about reuniting. It took some convincing, but we did it. We ended up doing a whole West Coast tour and, from there, we didn't stop.

EARL HUDSON

Soul Brains started because we wanted to appease H with changing the name. He wanted to change the name. He didn't want that connotation of bad even though we all know bad, meaning good, is tough. But he didn't think that's what people thought it meant. This is when Noel came into play, so we called it Soul Brains and we were still doing rock and reggae.

NOEL BAKER

H.R. was in a stable place with stable people and he could trust somebody to do his business and conduct it the way it needed to be done. I think that he wanted to see those guys and he wanted to bring money back to the band and to himself. Some of this is just to entertain himself and see how far he can push authority with a punk rock attitude, and some of it is a little insanity. He just likes to push the envelope. He likes the shock value.

He'd go out on these little adventures. H.R. had a video camera for a while. He shot all these videos of himself roaming around the subways, and singing and observing things. He just takes in the world. He's an eccentric individual and a lot of people would just stop and talk to him. He'd meet with people he hadn't seen in a while. I've seen him do it all day long.

NORWOOD FISHER

I didn't exactly know what was going on, but rumor had it he was going from place to place. I'd see him on the streets and I'm like, "Hey, that's H.R. Get in the car man, get in the car. Let's go." We had our studio called the Nutsack, and we were like, "Come on with us, we'll just go to the Nutsack." It was a period where he was wearing one white glove or a silver glove, and he was dressed like a general. He stayed at the studio for a minute. It made me think about the Bad Brains song "Big Takeover." He was exercising that right. I'd heard a lot of stories about him going and staying at people's houses. Next thing you know, he's fucking the dude's girlfriend, acting like, *It's my house*, until they got him out. He was doing the "Big Takeover."

CHINO MORENO

H.R. does things how he wants to. As many times as I've hung out with him, I was never able to pinpoint what is up with him. I've never seen the dude drugged-out or anything. He's an introvert and just doing his thing. We were in Malibu where we rented this place for three or four months. Deftones were writing a couple of records. He came out there and stayed with us for a week and every morning he'd get up, eat some cereal and just kick it. Just talking, very normal, and when it was time for us to rehearse, he'd strap his guitar on and just sit and hang. It was like having another band member. We actually recorded some vocals with him that could maybe be made into something. We had one track called "Pink Cell Phone," which was very cool.

TOBY MORSE

We played a show with Soul Brains in Japan and some of the shows go really late over there. It was us, MC Hammer, De La Soul, Dancehall Crashers and Bad Brains. They weren't going on until five in the morning. All the kids were lying over the barricade, falling asleep, but all of the American bands on the bill were so hyped to see them right up front. Me and my wife were so jet-lagged and tired, and we're like, "I don't think we're gonna make it. Let's go back to the hotel and chill for a little bit." As we're coming into the hotel, the elevator opens up and H.R. comes out with what looked like a birdcage on his head and a guitar. He looked at me and my wife and said "Peace and blessings" to us. It almost seemed like he floated out of the elevator and floated towards us. I swear to God. Me and my wife looked at each other and said, "We're staying," and jumped in the shuttle van with him and went back and watched Soul Brains. Something about him is surreal. Even if he's onstage playing a guitar that's not plugged in, I don't care, it's H.R. and he's amazing.

SONNY SANDOVAL

When I first met H.R., he came to the studio to be on our record. He came in with this huge Haile Selassie headdress and this cage with some birds up in there, some parakeets.

He's very soft spoken; he's not a blabbermouth; he's not telling everybody what's up. So it's like, *Did he bring these birds on purpose? Why did he do that? Is he crazy or is he making a point? What's going on?* I'm sure he was wilder and crazier back in the day, but for all the years that I've been privileged to know him, he's always listening and paying attention to what's going on—very reserved. And I think that's a matter of respect.

H.R.

The kind of music we were playing, people didn't want to gamble with that, so it took a little extra effort and a little more time than we had originally anticipated to get things going. Some people were leery of us and didn't want any part of the group or me. Then, after bouncing around and hitting my head against the wall, I said, "I can't take it anymore. Please, Jah, help me." And I would pray, and the Lord said, "Okay, I will provide for you." The Lord was saying he wanted to see if this was authentically part of my reality. "Did you, in your heart, really understand the message of Rasta?" The Spirit said, "Yes, I believe in you. You passed the test, now go on and reform the group." And I did.

ANTHONY COUNTEY

We played a couple of shows at CBGB just before it closed down, and it was whatever. That was before the band signed with Megaforce Records and did *Build a Nation*, which was produced by Adam Yauch. It took Megaforce wanting to do a deal and Mandy Stein wanting to make her Bad Brains movie. Those were the things that stimulated it back into existence. It's like the scene at the beginning of the Fellini film *8½*: He's in a traffic jam, and he starts floating away. Some people have got him by his toe—the string on his toe—and he's floating into the sky, and they start pulling him back. That's what we're doing with H.R. He's floating away, so we found things that gave it enough weight that he came back and joined us. At that point, he was still living in that warehouse in Baltimore. Actually, I think him living in Baltimore was an improvement from him staying in LA. He was getting back towards home. I didn't really know the situation that he was in.

H.R.

When I had just come back from LA, I started playing music with some people. Pablo Fiasco had a warehouse, and he opened his doors there for me. I was kind of homeless. For me, it was a test. I knew it was temporary. I knew I could do better for myself. I was selling out arenas, but at the same time, the arenas were selling me out because I still had to find a place to live. It was horrible over there by that warehouse. I didn't like living over there. That's when I started having these headaches. I didn't want to have headaches, and I didn't want to live in that warehouse. I didn't want to go through any of that kind of stuff.

ALLAN AGUIRRE

How do you go from being the front man of Bad Brains and Human Rights to absolute destitution in a warehouse in the ghetto? Obviously, now we know there was something really wrong going on. I think it's a combination of things. There could be too many drugs. I didn't know of anything but pot—so any rumors about other substances, I have no first-hand knowledge. If you smoke, eventually it's gonna catch up with you. Also, you have no clue about the business or handling of your money. You don't have people working for you in your best interest, as far as helping you navigate the waters of business. Money or publishing or royalties. Unfortunately, there are a lot of sharks out there who will absolutely, if they can, take advantage of you and take your money if you don't know any better. In addition, you've made bad choices in practical life scenarios, all your friends and family have abandoned you, you're on your own, and you're not in a healthy state of mind. Finding yourself locked away in a warehouse in Baltimore just doesn't happen. You have to be in a delusional state of being to allow people to put you away until they need you—like you're a pet or something. *Okay, let him out, cash in, do your thing, put him back in the cage.* Apparently, that's what was going on.

KENNY DREAD

There might be a relationship between his "I'm not gonna sign on this dotted line and do this big corporate thing" and his purposeful lifestyle; stay-on-the-edge, marginal living; and homelessness. I believe there may be a way to lean into that way of living, to keep yourself alive and also keep yourself fighting spiritually. We all, in the Dread House, our tribe dispersed, and H.R.'s homelessness was mirrored by many people in our crew; people lived on the road, people lived in squats, people lived in vans, people died and people went to jail. We all had a hard time adjusting. Life changed for all of us, and we all dealt with it in different ways. I think H.R. may have stayed true to it by being a rocker, living marginally a lot of the time.

15. HOUSE OF SUFFERING/ I AND I SURVIVE 2013 AND BEYOND

I think your spirit either goes up to Zion with Jah and the holy angels, or it goes on an endless journey through time and space. I look forward to being with the angels.

-H.R.

SKEETER THOMPSON

I was at those Howard Theatre shows in 2012. The Brains had two nights with GZA from Wu-Tang Clan. The band was just fucking great. Blown away, but Joseph . . . I was really let down. We had been talking before the show, and I was, like, "Are you going to give them a good show?" Everybody was having a great time. Joseph was in a great mood. And

about the fourth or fifth song, he sort of gave up. He just got into his own little shell. At first, I let it go, and then I was like, *Man, this is bullshit!* After the show, we went back down there and hung out. And I was like, "Dude, that's not acceptable." And he's like, "Why?" I said, "It's not fair to a lot of people out there who have never seen you guys, and you're sitting up there acting like the mic don't work. I was standing right up front. I know that mic was working." And he did this little, you know, *whatever* shrug. After the show, some words were exchanged, and the band was pissed for good reason.

JAMIE MITCHELL

Whatever we suffered from his episodes, Darryl, Dr. Know and Earl have suffered ten thousand–fold. To have your whole career depend upon the mental state of someone who is having episodes like that and basically forcing you into obscurity. I really feel for those guys. Man, if he were standing next to us today, I would just hug him. If I had anything to say to him, it would be, "To thine own self be true." As long as he is true to himself about what's real, then I'm fine with that. And I would really, really pray for him. Forget about the music and the career and bills and all that. I just want him to be a happy and healthy person. He has a whole family. Let's let him be a dad and a grandpa, just a happy member of the community. I think that's the bottom line for us today. We hope one day we hear about him painting on a beach somewhere or playing some guitar, doing whatever he wants to do. As long as he's a happy and healthy man.

H.R.

I don't think I'll perform or sing with Bad Brains again.

MARK ANDERSEN

There had definitely been an edge of madness around him, especially in the '80s and into the '90s. "The sunglasses era" is what I call it. I was, like, *Something's not right here. This is really worrisome. He's not there anymore.* Something happened to H.R. Something happened to Joseph. It was a mystery to me. I thought maybe something was done to him. Maybe it's mental illness. Some people would justify his eccentricities as, "This is just H.R. This is just how genius operates." I can buy it to a certain extent, but I'm sorry, I don't think genius is madness. I think madness is madness. And in a sense, I think H.R. is struggling with madness. He's struggling in a way that makes it less dangerous for those around him, but arguably more dangerous in the end for himself. Because I think there is this kind of "using people and being used by them" sick kind of dynamic around him. But mostly I think you get into the dance with the wrong people, and it's a dance of death. Again, it's just not the death of his tremendous artistic gift, it's a physical and spiritual death of this extraordinary person. This person I would rank in maybe the top ten of people who have transformed my life, that have inspired me to try and stretch beyond what is and what can be. This is no small thing.

ANGELO MOORE

Sometimes, man, you just got to wig out! Sometimes you've got to go there; you have to go to a different place as an artist. Maybe H.R. needs to enhance that somebody else in him at the moment that he puts his wig on. That's why I do it. It's like another character in me that I want to enhance, another personality. I just might throw a wig on. Maybe that's why H.R. does it, too. Sometimes it's just got to come out in the different flavors of H.R. He has a lot of different flavors. Sometimes they come out in his voice, and sometimes they come out in his fashion. I don't think H.R. really cares about money as a priority. He's just a spiritual guy, and he's happy to have a roof over his head, food in his mouth and clothes on his back.

SAUL WILLIAMS

If George Clinton put on that same wig H.R. had on, people would be, like, "Oh, that's George Clinton." When you start labeling things "good" and "bad," you create the avenue of good and bad, like when you start calling things beautiful, that leaves space for other things to become ugly or vice versa. It doesn't have to be that way. It can be a challenge to go there and to touch that. James Brown, for example, went someplace, too, but he kept the support of a band, and he kept it tight and dictated it. George Clinton touched on something with Bootsy. I mean, this is connected to James Brown. Bootsy left the JBs and went and hung out with someone his own age, George Clinton, and they created the

funk. He had people on the Mothership with him. But H.R. was a pioneer in a field, where he was left completely alone.

YANA CHUPENKO | PMS, WENCH

Weird, erratic behavior—everybody noticed that. "Eccentric," you would say. The eccentricity turned into a bit more of insanity—and I say that with love. There's nothing shameful about having mental issues as long as you seek help and you don't start killing people, you know what I mean? Coming out in weird clothes and wigs and refusing to sing . . . just sitting there onstage. Because I loved him and the band so much, I was sad and I couldn't watch the destruction of a human being in front of me—someone I cared for and who has meant so much to me and my life. It got to be uncomfortably weird.

VERNON REID

People always talk about living in the light, but you don't have light without darkness. Darkness defines what light

is. Without that, you have blinding nothingness. I don't know what normal is. A lot of us just find a way to get through the day. The voices come, and we don't listen to them. We have this thing, this range of behavior, this range of seeing things. That's what normal is. Outside of that, you're eccentric. Outside of that, you're mentally ill. I don't even know if there is a line.

One of the greatest things I've ever heard is "Talent is a symptom." When I heard that, I thought, *Exactly.* What drives us to create? Why do you need to be onstage? Why does somebody need to tell a joke or sing a song? With sports, everybody's on the team, but everybody's on the team for different reasons. One person loves the game. One person's trying to prove something to their dad. Somebody's trying to live up to what their grandfather did. Another person is trying to just make money. And they're all on the team at the same time. The answer can only come from H.R.

JOHN STABB

I've wondered, *is it just cashing in and making a chunk of money?* People in the band, it seems, over the years, have never really been able to quit their day jobs. It's like, why is the band pursuing this? Why is the band continuing this if they *know* that he's just going to give a half-assed performance? Why put out another record with this guy, whom they know is going to drive them crazy on the road? Is it an ego thing? Is it simply for the money?

JOHN JOSEPH

I just want to keep my shit positive about him. I remember the exact moment when I was like, *What the fuck?* But I don't really want to talk about that. Every man has his struggles. That's what life's about. To get to the next plateau, there's always gonna be a test put in front of you, and each time, you have to pass that test. All of this is part of his evolution. He's got a lot of support around him. Nothing changes with him and me. Any conversation that's ever been off between me and him, I don't take that personally. You can't.

IAN MACKAYE

Nobody would complain about H.R.'s more recent performances if they weren't doing shows. So maybe the question is: should he be doing shows? If you're gonna go out and call yourself the Bad Brains, and you're gonna stand like a statue in the middle of the stage and not acknowledge anybody, wear a scarf over your face . . . also, those shows are not cheap. People are being brought in to see the Bad Brains, and they have an idea of what the Bad Brains are. So if they go see the show and pay $24, and somebody doesn't want to perform that night, then people get discouraged.

EARL HUDSON

I think he went more on the introverted side of things when he moved out to California and started acting weird and shit. I don't know what happened out there. It's mysterious. Certain mental illnesses don't happen until a certain age. Maybe there's a chemical imbalance or a drug-induced whatever. Shit catches up with you. Prior drug use or whatever, man. That's probably what kicked in after a certain age. I'm not a psychologist or a doctor, so I can't really analyze it to the point where it would make any sense. God bless him, and thank you, Lord. He's married now, so hopefully she'll hang in there for him and keep him kind of level. All you can do is pray.

JAMIE MITCHELL

I think Joseph had a little bit of schizoaffective disorder. My stepdad is a neurologist. He's retired now, but Joe wanted to go see my dad and I wasn't able to make that happen. I still feel really guilty about it to this day. There were a couple things that happened, like I would come back from my lady's pad, and he would have his clothes hanging above the stove and he had the burners on. So I walked up to the door, and there was all this condensation on the front bay window, and I was like, *What is that?* I got inside, and it was like 110 degrees in there. He had the heater on and clothes drying above the stove.

JIMMY GESTAPO

Nobody goes onstage with a gold helmet and a bird. It's apples and oranges now. We toured with them for a couple of weeks a few years back. I saw the shows, and he would come out and just stand there and smile at the crowd. But not smile at the crowd like, "Hey, how are you doing?" But smile at the crowd like, beyond the crowd. He was coming from another place. The band was playing with their full spirit and full soul: the Bad Brains playing. The singer was not whom he used to be, and he was pulling out a Bible and reading—literally, he was reading the Bible—and people were leaving very unhappy. It went on for a couple shows, and I remember that Ian MacKaye was there. I don't know what dialogue went on between them, but H.R. came out. Somehow, he went back to being H.R. and it was fucking amazing! I will take that moment—and I did. I remember seeing Ian MacKaye and giving him a hug. Like, this is great and you're great. I'm sure there are a lot of people helping him, and God bless them.

KEITH MORRIS

The older guys don't really have to prove anything. H.R. has done backflips and the flying around. He's worn the wigs. He's worn the handcuffs. He's stood there and not moved. He's stood there saying all of the wrong lyrics. He's the guy that has earned the right to do whatever he wants to do. The light that I shine on H.R. is more of a humorous, comical light because we have all heard the horror stories. We have heard about the guy doing this and doing that bad thing, hitting this person. I'm going to tell a good story. I rarely get to see H.R., and when I do, I am extremely happy and I am extremely excited, because he's just one of those characters. I ran into him at the El Rey Theater on Wilshire Boulevard. The show was over, and he's just lounging on four folding chairs, licking on a lollipop. I'm looking at him and I'm going, *That's H.R. That's the gentleman that's one of the greatest lead singers of all time in an Elizabeth Taylor playing Cleopatra role.* Just lounging there, taking up space, looking at me like, "That's right, look at me. I'm black and I'm beautiful." Big Cheshire Cat smile on his face. I don't know if it's in his DNA to be crazy. Maybe it's something that he consumes. Maybe more north pole versus south pole. The only person that really knows is H.R.

ERIC WILSON

A lot of the best songwriters to ever live are crazy as hell with mental illness. I think he's been battling that since day one. My brother was schizophrenic and jumped off a building. I definitely know what it's like. He wasn't comfortable in his skin. Whatever H.R. I can get is awesome. For most people I know that have mental illness, drugs seem to bring out the worst in them. It did for my brother. I heard H.R. was on crack for a long time. I've never personally seen him smoke crack. I've smelled it in the vicinity, but anybody could have been smoking it.

CHUCK TREECE

I think most of us entertain two emotional societies: the real one and the not so real one. Then, all of a sudden, you become a public personality and you have to decide what side you can stand on. If someone's always watching you, watching what you say, what you do, listening to your records and reading your lyrics, when do you have time to make an honest mistake or experience something your everyday person would experience, the way they're able to experience it because they're not in the limelight? I don't know if Darryl and Doc are done with him. When I was with Darryl, even if he's bummed out about it, he always admits, "That's my big brother."

GUY OSEARY

After that incident on the Beastie Boys tour, I remember Freddy DeMann, whom I worked with, said, "I have experience with these guys. It's rock 'n' roll, things happen. Bring him in and let me talk to him. We'll get it worked out. Back on tour with the Beasties." So H.R. came in, and I remember Freddy giving him a great speech, very inspirational and supportive, and I saw H.R. actually get it. He said, "Freddy, I really appreciate that, and I will do whatever it takes to go back out there and do the right thing." And I was like, *Wow, this is amazing. This is going to start working out.* And then he goes, "Freddy, I have one question for you. When you were jamming with Jimi Hendrix and you were jamming with all the greats, what was it like?" He continued talking to him about something that made absolutely no sense, and so we knew that this wasn't going to work out.

I have no problem with an artist who wants to rock the boat and push down barriers. I don't have a problem with that. His problem was more with what was probably schizophrenia. That's just one piece of it. When I first got his number and I went to meet with him, he was living in some really small hole in the wall. Obviously, I knew he hadn't made any money in a long time. If you hear the albums, you think This guy's together. This guy's just a rebel. Nothing alluded to the fact that this guy had some serious mental issues.

CHINO MORENO

I don't like to look at it like he once was H.R. and now he's

not. I still believe that he is H.R. I think he has an odd way of how he wants to be perceived. I like to look at the positive side of it all, the things that I got from him that inspired me. What artist today is what they were in their prime? It's gotta be hard for the other guys in Bad Brains. I've never met the same H.R. twice. Although it's physically him, it just depends on the day or the moment he's in.

JACK RABID

I don't know what drugs have been prescribed to him to

keep him in a sort of pleased state. I know he went through a period when he was apparently very violent. These are things that I have heard and not seen. I am not a witness to these events. I've heard of them, and some of them are well-documented. I assume that he has been given some sort of drugs to curb that violent impulse that he had. He is friendly, and he is encouraging. But he is sort of distant and vacant, as if he is looking at puppies and ice cream and flowers somewhere in the back of his head. I didn't know Brian Wilson, but I guess if you were a friend of his in 1966 and you talked to him now, you'd see a shell of your former friend.

WILLIAM BANKS

He told me that he had an uncle or some family member from Jamaica who was off-center. That's how he explained it to me at one time. He was trying to say it was a gene thing from one of his family members and they were what people might call "nuts." But it could be the drugs and the things that people used to do. You can become imbalanced once you get off of certain things. It could be manic depression, because musicians get that way.

AL "JUDAH" WALKER

I'm gonna be honest with you, and I've said it a thousand times, I honestly believe that Joe was spiked. Spiked in his food or his weed, and the reason I'm saying that is because all the times I toured with him all over the country, we'd always have groupies around in the dressing room, and they would always have some kind of exotic weed already rolled, and he'd just smoke it. When they gave it to me I wouldn't do that, because I wouldn't know what they had in it. I'd just

put it in my shirt pocket. Anybody who knew him before he became ill with this schizophrenia thing knows all the good he's done for many people. He thinks about everybody before himself. A real friend, you don't have to really ask for help; they'll see that you need it and they'll give it to you. When you're doing good, they applaud you and they're with you. And when you're not doing so good, people just write you off as being worthless and somebody they don't want to relate to. If people would show the love that Joe showed everybody, maybe the power of that love could work miracles with his chemical imbalance to bring him back.

RON ST. GERMAIN

When you're mixing Molotov cocktails together, you know, you pay your money and you take your chances. And if you're on the edge with any kind of psychological thing, you're not stable. I knew people in college who would take LSD and never come back. Diving out of second-story windows, winding up in the emergency room, having psychotic events, and had to mainline Thorazine for three days to get their shit back together but never really quite recover.

ALLAN AGUIRRE

I remember seeing a flier for a Human Rights show, and they were actually boasting on the flier: "Making sure H.R. gets to the show for five years in a row." I was like, *Wow! What the hell is going on?* There's gotta be bad stuff going on if these guys are promoting, "We got H.R. to the show." 'Cause I remember, he would not show up for some shows. I would wait onstage, and he's not shown up, and now we got to kill time. "Those guys in San Gabriel, the 12 Tribes, he could be with them." And he wouldn't show up to Bad Brains shows. It started getting worse. That may be the reason these guys said that on a flier, but there was something else going on, obviously. Now we know there was something really wrong going on.

NOEL BAKER

He got on an airplane, and he's about two hours into the flight. He gets into the overhead compartment and pulls out a bulletproof vest and throws that on. It freaked out everybody on the airplane. The plane had to turn around, and he was met at the airport by sky marshals and all types of people until they could clear his identity.

ANGELO MOORE

Maybe he's scared of the beast. The beast can be considered record companies, record deals, the government, major establishments and things of that nature. Get you locked up in a contract that you can't get out of for a real long time. I remember one time he was playing at the House of Blues in LA and he had a duffle bag right in front of the monitors while he was doing his show. He picked up his duffle bag and left when he was done. He had all his belongings with him. You have to look at it as savant genius. If you have someone with a free spirit who is constantly expressing their different

personalities through the music and art, that's what H.R. does. He does it uncut. He lives it. It's good. I wanna express myself like that, too. I remember another time he was sitting out in front of Pablo's house with a sword, dressed like Sir Lancelot, with a little doll on his knee. I don't know if he was guarding Pablo's house, or if he wasn't gonna let Pablo into his own house. Schizophrenia is like a filter for your music and art. I think that's where you get the magic. You get the magic happening, but it's also not so great at times either. Everybody's got a little crazy shit about them, but if your heart is good and your intentions are good, then God will make a way for you somehow.

LORI CARNS HUDSON

I met H.R. in Baltimore. I was going out to see the Fishbone documentary, and he was having a show across the street. I was there with one of my friends and this man walked in, and I was, like, *Oh, my God, is that H.R.?* He walked right by me and our eyes met. It was almost as if we knew each other. A friend of my other friend knew him and introduced us. H.R. showed up to the after-party and I sat by him. We danced together and we talked. It was a beautiful evening. I was just happy that I met H.R.

I kept in touch with other people who knew him and just started showing up where he was, just because I was fascinated by him. I think he had just moved into Pablo Fiasco's house, and I was kind of getting to know the situation. People were taking care of him, but I think his mental state was so stressful that he just didn't know how to deal with it. I just felt from my heart that I was someone that could fill some gaps in his life. I had no idea where any of that would go.

H.R. and I were dating for only a few months when we decided to get married. As with any couple, the fact that we rushed it was looked down upon by certain people. I married him for the reasons you marry anyone. I loved him and wanted to be with him, and also I knew that if we were legally married I could get him more help. I could add him to my insurance and get him to the doctor. He decided he wanted to get married on Halloween. Not because he is a fan of Halloween. It's harvest time, I don't know. We got dressed up and went to Annapolis and got married. It was kind of a bittersweet day for me. He was not in the best mental state that day. He would not take his sunglasses off, but it was still happy in the end.

When Bad Brains were going to play Lollapalooza in South America, I wasn't happy about the fact that he was going. He did the shows and they were horrible. He was obviously hallucinating on the stage during the shows. He came back, and I think it was the moment when the rest of the band said, *This is enough. We can't put him on the stage like this anymore.*

ANTHONY COUNTEY

After South America, that's when he realized that he needed real help. To me, that was the first time that he basically was talking about another universe, and I was like, "If there is one thing happening here that you have to know, it is that there is only one universe. Whatever you are imagining, you are only imagining. You are still in this universe, and we are in the same universe." That kind of brought him around, too. That's when he realized that some of the stuff that he was paying attention to was not happening. It was just his imagination. Since then he has been getting help, and it's just a matter of time before he's able to do what he wants to do.

LORI CARNS HUDSON

It was very soon after I met him and started spending time with him when I recognized that there were some psychiatric issues. It was obvious to me. I didn't know if anyone had tried to help him with that before. I was just coming into a new situation. It's just that I wanted to help him in every way that I could, coming from a place of love. I sat down and went on some psychiatric website, and I read him all of the signs and symptoms for schizophrenia. I went down the list, and I read them all to him. "You do all of those. This is you. I know there is a stigma attached to it and nobody wants to admit that about themselves, but I want you to know that I love you no matter what, and this is what is going on with you, and there are things out there that can help you be able to function better."

Then Anthony Countey had some conversations with him. It took a while for it to sink in. Even if he doesn't react well to something that I'm saying to him, he is thinking about it and he comes back when he's ready to talk more. One day he said, "Okay, I'll do it. I'll go to the doctor." The first appointment, he got scared and didn't go. I called the doctor crying and she talked to him on the phone and she made

him, I guess, trust that it would be okay. His imagination was going all over the place with what it meant to go see a psychiatrist. She showed him it was just sitting down and talking, which it was, so that's how we got there.

He started taking the medication, and the doctor told us that the longer he took it, the better his symptoms would be, which has definitely turned out to be true. There was a period of time where I thought, *No, it's not working. We have to try to find the right dose.* There were so many ups and downs. He would be totally clear for two weeks, and then all of a sudden, it felt like he was back to before. We just kept going back to see her and talking things through. She was very encouraging to both of us, which I needed. I haven't seen him in psychosis in a long time. Occasionally, I'll see a little something behind his eyes, something that looks a little strange. I can see it right away because I know him so well. I see him every single day, and if something is a little off, I can tell. And so I can deal with it and give him extra medicine or whatever he needs. He's himself now. He wasn't himself for so long.

He's a quiet, kind person. He likes to spend a lot of time alone or just with me. That's just the way he is. He's happy and he smiles all the time. It's great to see him that way. Other people in his life who have seen the changes are really psyched for him, too, of course. The healing process began long before I met him, when he decided to stop smoking herb. He decided that on his own. Somehow he knew inside of him that that wasn't good for him anymore. When I met him, I talked to him about herbal medicine, nutrition and organic food and everything like that. I tried to get his body healthier, too. He was eating Ramen noodles and breads and that was it. You have to heal from the inside out. Your body, your spirit and your mind alltogether. Once he started taking the medication he definitely had times where he was like, "I'm not doing this anymore," and I was like, "Yes, you are." He is completely dedicated. He is not going to stop taking that medication. He really sees the benefit that it has for him.

JUAN DECOSTA

I was there. How many people can say that they were there with Bad Brains? How many muthafuckas slept on the roof with Joseph? We used to break bread together. Joe taught me how to eat natural food. It wasn't even popular back then. Joe taught me how to take care of myself. If you're looking at me, you see a piece of Joe. My life is good because of Joseph. He's never alone because the Lord will always be with Joseph. You come in here by yourself and you leave by yourself, but let me tell you, that dude's like a cat with nine lives. He always lands on his feet. Joe is alright, man. Joe is all right. Just find some peace with yourself, man. The fight is over, man. And guess what? We won.

ANTHONY COUNTEY

H.R. is definitely a success. He was real for people who needed him to be real and that's much more important than anything else. He survived those days he was living in a warehouse. H.R. was the protector of the spirit of it all, and in order to protect that spirit he had to kill the dragon over and over. It's about what's on those records and what was at those shows. All the rest is just talk.

EARL HUDSON

H.R. is my brother. We're family so there's nothing that's gonna destroy that. There have been certain times when he's lifted me up, and if there's anything I can do for him, then I have do that for him. He knows that. That's why he came back to do Bad Brains, so I could eat food, too—so we could all eat food. Him, Darryl, Gary, and I are all brothers, in essence. He's like our oldest brother. We all love H.R. because we remember how he was back in the days. We all starved and ate together and cried together and everything. He is a contributing factor to why the Bad Brains happened and why this music is so profound in America these days—because of all his work, writing lyrics and the positiveness that he did bring to the music.

LORI CARNS HUDSON

I want to make sure people know that H.R. is not all of the things he has done wrong in his past. That has nothing to do with who he is at this moment. Everybody has a past. We have all done stupid shit. He has done a lot of stupid shit, but he is not that. Who he is for real is a sincere, genuine, creative, beautiful spirit, and that's why I married him, and that's why I'm with him. He's not perfect. A lot of people call him a prophet, and that's great if that works for you. I'm sure he's helped a lot of people through his music. I do not see him that way. He is my husband, but I understand. I was a fan of his before I met him. I'm still a fan of his, just in a very different way. Sometimes I look at him and honestly I just think, *How am I sitting here with H.R.?* It would just be great if everyone could put aside things from the past or ideas that they have created about him and try to see him as the real person that he is. If I can make H.R. laugh, deep belly laughs, then I know how

happy he is—and that is everything right there.

H.R.

The lady at the hospital told me I had to remember that people who do not sleep are always going through changes. And when I went to that hospital and I started to get myself together, a big change came into my life. I want to thank all you guys for helping out too. The kids have always supported the Brains. I'll tell you the truth, the hospital helped me to become a better human being. It's a miracle that I'm alive because about ten years ago, one doctor analyzed me and said, "He's only got a few more months to live and then he's gone."

My life has been changed. It's all about how people can set an example with good things, and people can learn from it. It was a bad scene but now that I've been reborn again and have repented, it's a good scene. Read the bible to the fullest, come to grips with reality and one will be able to learn. I want to tell the musicians, and this is very important: keep your families together, keep your job and don't fuss and fight because it's not going to work.

Peace and blessings to each and everyone, and Merry Christmas and Happy New Year. Don't worry because the Lord is working in mysterious ways; where there is a will, there is a way and one can achieve whatever they do truly conceive and believe.

16. HERE I AM

There are countless tales of artists who've had to pick up the pieces of their lives and rebuild them. In certain instances, the rehabilitation is from addiction to alcohol or drugs. In others, it might be financial bankruptcy. In the case of H.R., there have been a multitude of complicated causes, many far beyond his control. For years, his mind and body were out of sync, and he coped as best he could. Thankfully, through his faith in God and the concern and generosity of friends and a devoted wife, he has persevered.

It is all too easy for those short on compassion to make light or make fun of people who suffer silently. So many who've witnessed H.R. on stage and off over the last several years have done both, devoid of any understanding of what this music giant was grappling with. Fans selfishly wanted the return of "backflip H.R." to entertain and enlighten them. It's tragic, yet somewhat understandable, perhaps even forgivable. Nonetheless, when all is said and done, H.R. is loved.

On pages 14–17 of this book, the conversation with H.R., who was struggling mightily to present anything comprehensibly, is a revealing document of the state of H.R.'s mind at that time. In some instances, his answers do not even address the questions. While some can be viewed as comic or absurdist responses, they actually reveal the effects of mental illness brought about by an acute condition. H.R. was still in the throes of a battle with mental illness, and was soon to confront debilitating headaches, later diagnosed as SUNCT Syndrome (short-lasting unilateral neuralgiform headache with conjunctival injection and tearing). That was H.R. during the winter of 2012.

Below is a more recent conversation with H.R., alongside his wife Lori, which took place twenty-one months after a complicated brain surgery. Thanks largely to Lori, in addition to his own determination, H.R. is better and improving every day.

The following conversations took place between November 29 and December 6, 2018

HOWIE ABRAMS: How are you feeling these days?

H.R.: Oh man, much better. I was able to get some surgery done, and months later, the headaches went away. I'm working hard making music with Human Rights, and the Brains got back together and did a big show in Chicago at Riot Fest, which was remarkable. There were so many people and I wasn't sure I was ready for it. It was very inspirational and exciting. Then we had another show in California and that went great. The group really sounded great.

LORI CARNS HUDSON: He has been healing on every level. I've definitely noticed him not only having more physical energy and his voice getting stronger, but also his spirit. He's much more in the moment. He's more present. It's all just getting better. I'm so happy for him.

HOWIE: How did it feel to be back on stage with your brothers in Bad Brains?

H.R.: It felt miraculous. It was great to be working with Darryl, Gary and my brother again. In a sentimental way, it felt like, how do you know what you're going to do until you do it, you know? I mean, I'd heard through the grapevine that the Bad Brains were going to get together and play again, but it wasn't until I talked to Darryl and he said, "Please, come on man, come and work with the Brains again, come enjoy yourself," and I told him, "Of course, let's do it." Then I knew it was really going to happen. Darryl said, "I'm committed to you and whatever you want to do," and asked if I wanted to play reggae or hardcore, and I told him that I preferred to play reggae, so he told me to let him know which songs I wanted to play and we practiced those. That's how that happened.

HOWIE: You did wind up playing some of the hardcore songs at those shows.

H.R.: Yes, we did. It was a challenge. It was different because I've been playing reggae with my band Human Rights for years now, and it caught me by surprise. I thought we were going to play all reggae and, at the last minute, they asked if I would play one hardcore song, "FVK," and I said, "Sure, I'll give it a try." It was a big surprise. I had no idea how it was going to come off, but it sounded great.

HOWIE: Bad Brains did those shows with Randy Blythe from Lamb of God doing some of the set on vocals after you. What was that like for you?

H.R.: Randy had told me how much he liked those songs and the lyrics I had written. It was funny because before one of those shows, we were all in the hotel lobby and our rooms weren't ready. Randy invited us up to stay in his room, which I really appreciated. Lori had told me earlier that he sang in Lamb of God, and I knew he went through some trials and tribulations when he was in the Czech Republic. Watching him play with the other guys in the Brains was definitely different, but he seemed to really enjoy himself, so I said, "Cool runnings," you know.

HOWIE: Will there be new Bad Brains music sometime in the future?

H.R.: Oh, I don't know. That's in God's hands. It's his plan.

Howie: But you are working on new music with Human Rights?

H.R.: Yes. We're working on an album called We Are One which we're recording in Philadelphia. I'm working with a brother named Ezekiel Zagar who knew some musicians who played reggae and knew where we could record. He plays guitar and has even become my landlord, too. I have a place just above his studio. We auditioned musicians and now we have a maximum band and they sound so cool.

HOWIE: You recently performed in New York at the memorial for Todd Youth (Murphy's Law, Warzone) at Niagara which used to be A7. Was it strange to be back at one of the first venues you ever played in New York?

H.R.: We had played there a few times after the Brains came to New York. That was in the basement. It was interesting though because I had no idea Gary (Dr. Know) would be playing with me. I hadn't seen him since we did the Bad Brains show in California about two years earlier. I'd heard a rumor that he might be there, but nobody told me he was going to be playing guitar. Sure enough, he was there, and his wife played keyboards.

HOWIE: What is it about reggae music that makes you want to communicate through it?

H.R.: It's something the father wants me to do, the father on Mount Zion. He told me to try reggae and see what the reaction would be from the kids, and they let me know that they liked when I played reggae, even back when we played both reggae and rock 'n' roll. This music gives me joy in my heart and a purpose. There's a message of unity and to live in harmony; not to worry about your brother's color.

HOWIE: Are you surprised by the outpouring of love toward you since the release of the Finding Joseph I film and book?

H.R.: I sure am. I think people understood what I was going through and really showed their respects to me. I mean, we had a Kickstarter going to try to make the film, and the number of donations that came in surprised me. I think there were 450 people who contributed. Some gave twenty dollars, some gave fifty dollars. There was even one guy named Tero Viikari from Finland who helped out a lot and became a producer. It was amazing.

HOWIE: What has it been like looking back at your own life through the film and the book?

H.R.: It's been a little shocking hearing what all these people have had to say about me. I had no idea that people had such admiration for me. It's like, "WOW." I didn't know I was so liked by so many people. It's been exciting, and thrilling and wonderful at the same time.

HOWIE: But you've been playing shows to thousands of people for so many years; how come you're so surprised by this?

H.R.: Well, I guess because up until now, I didn't hear them tell me. Maybe they've told each other, you know, people in other bands or bandmates of mine, but they never really came up to me to let me know. I've been asked to play music with a lot of people, but they never just told me how much they liked me.

HOWIE: What about seeing and hearing about all your eccentric behavior over the last several years? Do you remember those times?

H.R.: I definitely remember. I stayed out in California for quite a while and was homeless for some of it. It was a different vibration. A brother named Marco took me in. He said, "Come take a shower, relax and eat some good food. I'll help you out." He got me off the streets, made sure I could get clean and got to rest, and I'm so thankful he did. During that time, I met so many people who saw what I was going through but didn't know how to help me. I did some singing gigs with groups like 311 and P.O.D., and it was quite an experience bouncing around from place to place like that, but I learned to put my faith in God and give him the power to transform me and help me out. He sure did. I remember when the Brains got that deal with Madonna and Maverick Records. I took my advance and went and bought a car.

HOWIE: The limo?

H.R.: Yeah, the limo. People were like, "You were just homeless, now you're driving a limo and have your own apartment." After we finished God of Love, we went on tour and me and the manager had a confrontation. We were on tour with the Beastie Boys and we didn't know where our money was at, and Anthony and I had that fight. The band eventually parted ways with him.

HOWIE: The concept of PMA gets thrown around a lot now, but the principle of it is very important to you. How have you applied PMA during your difficult times?

H.R.: Basically, I've just learned to put my faith in God and be positive. The theory that Napoleon Hill had in that book, Think and Grow Rich, made me rethink the negative things in my life and put them out of my mind, put my strength into being positive, and that's what I did. I worked the theory and put it into practice to see if it would really happen, and it happened. My life changed. Also, a lot of times the youth would come to me and tell me they understood what I was going through and to hold on. They gave me the will to survive and supported me and have a lot to do with this, me getting through the hard times. The youth understood.

HOWIE: You also stopped smoking ganja.

H.R.: Yes, I did. It's been about seven years. I had to make a decision: was I going to take care of my voice or keep smoking the herb, 'cause there was some strong reefer going around that kept me coughing. (LAUGHS.) I felt the strain on my vocal cords, and I didn't want to strain anymore. People still come up to me and want to share the herb, but I just say, "No, thank you." I know there are always going to be some temptations, but I told myself that I had to rise above those temptations. The youth can find out for themselves.

HOWIE: While you were homeless, you seemed to have represented a lot of different personalities; wearing strange clothing, wigs, etc. Was that you just having fun, something to help you get through the day, or what?

H.R.: It was mostly entertainment. I wanted to entertain people by trying things that were new and different, so I would switch up with costumes, wearing makeup and wigs. People would say, "That dude's schizophrenic with all the changes he's going through," but it was entertainment. My doctor told me that I'm quite a balanced young man.

HOWIE: How long did you suffer from debilitating headaches?

H.R.: Over five years.

HOWIE: Can you describe them?

H.R.: I felt them on the left side, by the temple. It was an excruciating feeling, sort of a stabbing sensation on my brain.

LORI: The headaches changed a lot since I've known him. They went from something he would get occasionally to something which would happen much more often. It culminated during the fall of 2015 when he was getting them all the time. The severity varied, but they always lasted a very long time.

HOWIE: What were you doing to try to ease the pain?

H.R.: I tried a few things, including acupuncture, but noting worked. Lori and I went to see several doctors, and they did different tests—blood work, an MRI. We wound up seeing a surgeon named Dr. Lee who suggested I was a candidate for brain surgery. He said something was resting on a nerve in the wrong way, and he would go in and clean that up.

LORI: He tried taking Tylenol and Ibuprofen. None of what people normally take for headaches worked. Then he began taking the sleep aid, Unisom. He thought it helped and kept taking it. I didn't see any positive result from him taking it. He kept telling himself that it was helping, but it didn't, and he wound up having a problem with the Unisom after a while. He had been taking them at all hours of the day. Also, he had been taking medicine for his mental health issues, and the Unisom was interacting with those medications. I had a really hard time explaining to him that he shouldn't be taking those together. I spent several years fighting with him about that until he finally stopped.

HOWIE: What was the next step?

LORI: It took months to get in to see a neurologist, and then we'd try to see another one and that took several more months. It was horrible. We went to see three different neurologists who tried different medications for the headaches, until we got into the Headache Center in Philadelphia. At first, he was diagnosed with two different things because his worst headaches were nocturnal. At his worst, he was getting them twenty-four hours a day, but they seemed to be worst at night. They gave him meds that made him wobbly and dizzy. He wasn't taking them as directed either—with food or at the certain times he was supposed to be taking them. At one point, he was admitted to the hospital where they gave him an in-patient lidocaine infusion, which was to try to numb the nerve, but he didn't react well to that. Some people do really well with that treatment, but he didn't. It helped a bit while he was there, but the effects didn't last.

After around six months, they had tried everything. His doctor suggested we reach out to a surgeon at a different hospital, so we began consulting with him. He showed us a video of a procedure usually done for trigeminal neuralgia patients. They go in through the skull to where the nerves are being compressed by blood vessels and insert a tiny barrier between the blood vessel and the nerve to remove the pressure. Originally, the MRI showed only one nerve being compressed, but during the surgery, the surgeon noticed that there were two compressed nerves, so two barriers were inserted. While they didn't actually touch H.R.'s brain during the surgery, because they have to cut into the skull next to the brain, it's considered brain surgery.

HOWIE: What was the day of the surgery like?

H.R.: I was pretty strong. I was ready for it. I had been told to brace myself, so that's what I did, even though I didn't really know what was going to happen. Before the surgery, Lori was there with me, and said to me, "Don't worry, we're here with you. Everything's going to be all right." I had been through so much, and I didn't know if this was going to work, but Dr. Lee told me to relax and then he put me under anesthesia. I was like, Okay, here we go! I just wanted this to be solved.

LORI: He was mostly calm, but he was scared, of course. It's terrifying to know someone's going to be cutting your skull open, but he handled it really well. We had to get up early in the morning, which helped because we didn't have to sit around all day waiting. We just got up and went. We arrived there; he went into the surgical prep area and got ready. I was sitting there with him, holding his hand, and he remained as calm as a person can in that situation. He was saying that he couldn't wait until it was over.

HOWIE: How did you feel after the surgery?

H.R.: I was still having some headaches, but they became weaker and weaker and came less often, until after several months, they finally went away.

LORI: Immediately afterward, there wasn't much of a difference. There was so much swelling, so there wasn't any immediate relief. It was heartbreaking to have to watch him heal from the surgery while still having headaches. That was really hard, and I was like, "It didn't work, it didn't work." I was trying not to say that to him, and I kept telling him that we had to wait as the doctor said. It was very hard not knowing what was going to happen. After maybe three months, the headaches began to come less frequently. It took a few months before he really had a break, but then he would start getting them again. The doctors told us that they were hoping for a seventy-percent reduction in his headaches. We went to our follow-up with the surgeon and he seemed happy with the progress, even though he was still having headaches. He had a show around seven months after the surgery, and it was pretty good, but he got a headache earlier that day which made me worry. After that, there were much greater stretches of time between headaches, and they were much less severe. The last one he ever had was on Christmas Day 2017. No one knew but me, but he just handled it. That was the last one.

HOWIE: How has Lori helped you through all of this?

H.R.: Well, a few months after we got married, Lori's the one who said, "Look, you keep having these headaches. Let's go to a hospital and see what they can do." God bless her soul. She's been patient with me and so very helpful. She encouraged me to stop dealing with all this hokey pokey and witchcraft stuff. (LAUGHS.) We decided to go about this more realistically and see doctors. Lori's a wise sister and got me to look at this in a wise way. She was hopeful and determined. At first, I was unsure about it all, but she pulled me through it and I thank God for her. She truly led me in the right direction.

LORI: For a long time, the headaches took everything out of him, and that was on top of untreated mental illness. It was impossible for him to be himself. Maybe a few days a month, I felt like I was talking to H.R. Every other day, he was somebody else and he was suffering, deeply suffering. It takes a long time to heal from that. We started seeing an extremely talented psychiatrist and she's gotten him on a really good balance of medication which has helped him. It's been a combination of his own healing and her help that has made his recovery possible. It's so wonderful.

HOWIE: And what about (Finding Joseph I director) James Lathos? How was working with him helpful?

H.R.: He came to me when I was living in that warehouse in Baltimore and wanted to do an interview. Later on, he asked me if I wanted to do a movie with him. At first, I didn't understand why he wanted to call it Finding Joseph I even though I had been called "Joseph I," but I found it exciting and very revealing. He told me to just be myself, and I got a chance to explain myself to people. I got to talk about different revelations, and I thank God for him. Through him, I met you, and I want to thank you, too, Howie. The film and the book let me see my struggles from the outside after experiencing them from the inside. I learned a lot about myself. I became more enlightened and inquisitive about what I was going through. I've read the Bible many times over, but now when I read it, I take it one chapter at a time and try to learn how it really relates to me. What's my message about? What should I do with it? Should I keep it to myself, or share it with people? I learned to put those words in with my own and share them.

HOWIE: What are you listening to these days?

H.R.: Mostly reggae: The Abyssinians, Desmond Dekker, Israel Vibration, lots of Bob Marley. These were all very influential for me, and I learned a lot from them. I learned that suffering makes you stronger, and that it's not going to last forever. Suffering made me understand what it takes to be a Rasta. It let me know that it may be bitter now, but it's going to be sweet later on.

HOWIE: What kind of advice do you have for people who may be struggling, or are unhappy with the way their lives are going?

H.R.: Well, I would tell them that even though things may look bad, like what we're going through with our president, Donald Trump—he's throwing down these ideas that people are not too sure about and putting them on the people—don't worry. Rise above it. Stick to your guns and do what feels right. I mean, I care about politics because it affects me, but I don't get involved in things like congressmen and vetoes. I don't worry myself with that. I don't get involved on that level.

HOWIE: You wear sunglasses all the time. Are you just cool like that, or do they help you see?

H.R.: (LAUGHS.) They are prescription, so they do actually help me see better.

CAST OF CHARACTERS

ALLAN AGUIRRE was a member of the short-lived Christian punk band Scaterd Few during the early '80s. He later played with H.R. around the time of the *Charge* album.

MARCO ALDACO is a friend of H.R.'s from Los Angeles, who looked after him upon finding H.R. homeless on Hollywood Boulevard in the mid-1990s.

MARK ANDERSEN is the cofounder of the activist/creative collective Positive Force DC, which was sparked by the '80s punk and hardcore scene in Washington, DC. He has published two outstanding books, *Dance of Days: Two Decades of Punk in the Nation's Capital* and *All The Power: Revolution Without Illusion*.

AL ANDERSON was a guitar player in The Original Wailers. He is the only musician to have played with both Bob Marley and H.R.

TERRY ANZALDO was the head of promotions at Maverick Records during the Bad Brains' time signed to the label.

NOEL BAKER was H.R.'s personal manager from 1998 to 2004.

WILLIAM BANKS appears on several of H.R.'s reggae recordings playing various instruments, including the short-lived *Zion Train* project.

JULIE BIRD is a cofounder of Olive Tree Records, which released titles by H.R., Beefeater and others.

RUSSELL BRAEN was the music manager at the Washington, DC, venue and artist collective Madam's Organ, where many DC-area bands played their earliest shows—H.R. and Bad Brains included.

JULIAN CAMBRIDGE is a musician and friend of H.R.'s from the early Bad Brains days and was integrally involved in H.R.'s move toward Rastafarianism.

RANDY CHOICE is a Washington, DC, native who played keyboards with H.R. during the early '90s, including the 1992 release *Our Faith*. He currently lives in Dublin, Ireland.

YANA CHUPENKO was a NYC hardcore scene staple and the dynamic lead vocalist in both PMS and Wench. She loves singing Dio songs.

ANTHONY COUNTEY began managing Bad Brains in 1982—and, by all accounts, he did so through 2013.

JUAN DECOSTA is an old friend of H.R.'s from the Madam's Organ days in DC.

KENNY DREAD played bass on several of H.R.'s reggae releases and lived in the Dread House, along with H.R. and many others. Kenny toured off and on with Human Rights up until 1989.

LARRY DREAD is a member of the group African Unity, and is featured on the *Rock Of Enoch* album. He has been a great friend to H.R. for many years.

ENGLISHMAN played bass with H.R.'s band on the *Charge* album.

NORWOOD FISHER, along with his brother Phillip "Fish" Fisher, founded the ska-punk-funk outfit Fishbone in 1979 in South Central Los Angeles. He plays the crap out of the bass.

MICHAEL FRANTI kicked off his music career in San Francisco, California, with art-punkers The Beatnigs; he moved on to The Disposable Heroes of Hiphoprisy; and he now makes moves with Michael Franti & Spearhead. He is a staunch advocate for peace and social awareness.

JIMMY GESTAPO, aka James Drescher, is a Queens, New York native and pioneer of the hardcore scene in New York City. He has fronted the band Murphy's Law since 1982 and is one of the funniest and wittiest gentlemen you could ever meet.

COREY GLOVER was born in Brooklyn, New York, and is the lead singer for Living Colour. He also played Francis in the film *Platoon*.

JOSE GONZALES was the first bass player in H.R.'s reggae group. He previously played with early NYHC purveyors The Mob.

STEVEN HANNER is a photographer who has captured many great moments throughout the career of H.R. and Bad Brains, including the iconic live image of the Brains from inside the packaging of the *I Against I* album.

MIGUEL HAPPOLDT founded Skunk Records and produced and performed in Sublime and Long Beach Dub Allstars. Miguel has also done production work for Slightly Stoopid and Unwritten Law.

NICK HEXUM was born in Madison, Wisconsin, and is the vocalist and guitarist for 311. Among other projects, Nick appeared on a track for *Chef Aid: The South Park Album,* alongside Flea and Tom Morello.

H.R., aka Joseph I, is the lead vocalist and lyricist for Bad Brains, Human Rights and Zion Train. He is the greatest front man of all time. H.R. is married and currently resides in Philadelphia, Pennsylvania.

EARL HUDSON is the drummer for Bad Brains, Human Rights and Zion Train. He is H.R.'s younger brother and an extraordinary skinsman.

LORI CARNS HUDSON is H.R.'s loving wife.

ILL BILL was born and raised in Brooklyn, New York, and is one of the finest independent rappers ever to come from the five boroughs. H.R. is featured on two of Bill's tracks: "Riya," on his *The Hour of Reprisal* album, and "Forty Deuce Hebrew" on *The Grimy Awards.*

RAKAA IRISCIENCE is a member of Los Angeles's alternative hip-hop outfit Dilated Peoples.

DEB JONES is originally from Australia, and worked with Bad Brains' manager Anthony Countey. She served as H.R.'s assistant during the *God of Love* album cycle.

DAVID JORDAN played guitar in H.R.'s band early on and is still convinced that H.R. owes him money.

ISRAEL JOSEPH I was the Bad Brains' vocalist for the *Rise* album and tour cycle.

JOHN JOSEPH is the front man for NYHC legends the Cro-Mags. He is also an author, having published the excellent *The Evolution of a Cro-Magnon* and also *Meat Is for Pussies*.

M-1 is one-half of the politically fueled hip-hop duo Dead Prez from NYC. DP's debut album in 2000, *Let's Get Free*, is an underground classic!

ALEC MACKAYE is the younger brother of Minor Threat and Fugazi front man Ian MacKaye and has been a member of Untouchables, The Faith and Ignition. Alec is whom you see on the cover of Minor Threat's classic self-titled EP.

IAN MACKAYE was the lead vocalist of Minor Threat and Fugazi as well as other groups, and he founded the incredible Dischord Records. Ian coined the term "straight edge," using it as the title for a song by the same name on Minor Threat's EP, *Minor Threat*.

SID MCCRAY is an early friend of the members of Bad Brains and was the man who turned them on to punk rock. He was Bad Brains' first singer but stepped aside to make way for H.R.

DUFF MCKAGAN is the bass player for Guns N' Roses and also played in Velvet Revolver. He saw Bad Brains play in Seattle, Washington, on their very first tour of America.

JAMIE MITCHELL was a member of H.R.'s band during the early 1990s and was also his roommate.

ANGELO MOORE, aka Dr. Madd Vibe, is the lead vocalist and saxophonist for the genre-bending outfit Fishbone. He lives in Los Angeles, California.

CHINO MORENO, born Camillo Wong Moreno, is the lead vocalist and occasional guitarist for Deftones. His other projects include Team Sleep, Crosses, Saudade and Palms.

KEITH MORRIS helped form the legendary Southern California hardcore band, Black Flag; was the front man for the Circle Jerks; and currently fronts both Off! and Flag.

TOBY MORSE is a ball of energy and fronts the tuneful NYHC band H2O. In addition, Toby does speaking engagements at schools across America under the banner "One Life, One Chance," in an effort to keep the youths positive and out of trouble.

OPIE ORTIZ is a member of Long Beach Dub Allstars and is a tattoo artist in Long Beach, California. He is the tattooer who inked the Sublime logo onto Bradley Nowell's back, which appears on the cover of the Sublime album. He also created the iconic sun artwork on Sublime's *40oz to Freedom* album, and can be seen on the cover of their *Robbin' the Hood* album.

GUY OSEARY was an A&R executive and, later, chairman of Madonna's Maverick Records. He signed Bad Brains to Maverick.

LUCIAN PERKINS is a photojournalist who captured a number of crucial gigs during the development of Washington, DC's, punk and hardcore scenes. His book, *Hard Art, DC 1979*, features incredible photographs from that early period in the District.

QUESTLOVE is the extraordinary percussionist for The Roots and appears every weeknight on *The Tonight Show Starring Jimmy Fallon*. He will expound upon the greatness and influence of H.R. and Bad Brains to anyone within earshot.

JACK RABID is the cofounder of the zine *The Big Takeover*, named after the Bad Brains song. He was a member of the early NYC punk band Even Worse with one-time Beastie Boy John Berry.

RAS MG/MARSHALL GOODMAN plays drums in Sublime as well as Long Beach Dub Allstars, which reformed in 2012.

RAS MICHAEL is a Jamaican reggae singer and Nyabinghi specialist. He played the role of guru to H.R. as he became more deeply involved with Rasta. In addition to acting as an evangelist, ambassador and diplomat for the Ethiopian Orthodox Tawahido Church, Ras Michael is a cofounder and president of the Rastafarian International/Marcus Garvey Cultural Center in Los Angeles, and the Fly Away Culture Center in Kingston, Jamaica. Currently, he lives in California.

VERNON REID is a guitarist, songwriter, composer and producer, best known for his work with the Grammy Award–winning band Living Colour. His collaborations outside of LC include everyone from Donald Byrd and Ronald Shannon Jackson to Public Enemy, Janet Jackson and Mick Jagger. Reid, like H.R., was born in the UK.

JIMI RILEY worked at Olive Tree Records as a graphic designer and became a close friend of H.R.'s while living in the Dread House. He and H.R. had a well-documented falling out, which went a step further when Jimi interviewed H.R. for the *WDC Period* in 1985.

AL RONDON played drums as a member of The Crabiteers, which backed up H.R.'s reggae offerings during the early 1990s.

ANDY RONDON is Al's brother and was also the bassist in The Crabiteers.

SONNY SANDOVAL is the lead vocalist for the San Diego, California, rap-metal band P.O.D. (Payable on Death). He is a devout Christian and once tried his hand at being an MC.

JOHN STABB was best known as the vocalist for DC hardcore stalwarts Government Issue. John sadly passed away on May 7, 2016, at the age of fifty-four following a hard-fought battle with stomach cancer.

RON ST. GERMAIN produced the Bad Brains' stellar *I Against I* and *Quickness* albums and mixed their live album, *The Youth Are Getting Restless*. Ron's other credits include . . . pretty much anyone and everyone in the music business. Google it!

MO SUSSMAN managed Bad Brains until around 1981, when he and the band parted ways over a difference of philosophy as to the direction of the band.

SKEETER THOMPSON is the bassist for one of DC hardcore's finest bands, Scream.

ALVAREZ TOLSEN is a childhood friend of H.R.'s and has appeared on a handful of his recorded projects, including the *Charge* and *Singin' in the Heart* albums.

MARLANDO TOLSEN is Alvarez's brother, an early friend of H.R.'s.

CHUCK TREECE is an incredible multi-instrumentalist, originally from Newark, Delaware. He was the touring drummer for Bad Brains at one time and was a member of both McRad and Underdog. Chuck used to be a pro skateboarder and even played the bass line on Billy Joel's "The River of Dreams" single.

AL "JUDAH" WALKER is a vocalist/musician who has collaborated with H.R. on many of his reggae projects over the years.

SAUL WILLIAMS is an acclaimed hip-hop poet, musician and actor. He has starred in films and on Broadway and has had his poetry published by *The New York Times* and elsewhere.

ERIC WILSON was the bassist for Sublime and Long Beach Dub Allstars, among others, and currently handles the low end for Sublime with Rome.

CREDITS

Lyrics to "Happy Birthday My Son" reprinted with permission

INTERIOR & COVER DESIGN BY:
Donna McLeer / Tunnel Vizion Media, Brooklyn, NY

COVER PHOTOS:
Front: Steven Hanner
Back: D. Randall Blythe Taken from D. Randall Blythe's
forthcoming book Frontman

PHOTOGRAPHY CONTRIBUTED BY:
H.R
Jeff Schmale
Marcia Resnick
Lucian Perkins
James Mahoney
Steven Hanner
The Sussman Family
MJ Vilardi
Jamie Mitchell
Ken Salerno
Mateus Mondini
Miguel Happoldt
Rusty Moore
Trent Nelson
Lori Carns Hudson
James Lathos

H.R. logo images on endpapers contributed by Craig Ibarra.

ACKNOWLEDGEMENTS

H.R. WOULD LIKE TO THANK: Mom and Dad, Lori, my brother Earl, Bad Brains, Shamus, Howie, Small Axe Films and all of my friends.

JAMES LATHOS WOULD LIKE TO THANK: God, Sheila, Jordan, Mazzy, Jeff Schmale, Rob Parsell, Terry Anzaldo, Kevin McGuinness, Andrew Aaman, Miguel, Jay Mohr, Res, Howie, Small Axe Films, Post Hill Press and all my family and friends.

HOWIE ABRAMS WOULD LIKE TO THANK: James Lathos for being so gracious and dedicated to this project, Jacob Hoye and all at Post Hill Press, Marcus Turner, Peter Nussbaum, Donna McLeer, Michael Croland, Randi Klein and D. Randall Blythe.

To my dearest Julie and Nia: You are my light and my love!

Special Thanks to all who agreed to be interviewed and those who contributed photographs.

Extra Special Thanks and praises to the inimitable H.R. We are forever grateful for everything you have done and continue to do and all that you are, which is the greatest of all time.

Rest in Peace John Stabb and Mo Sussman.

ABOUT THE AUTHORS

HOWIE ABRAMS is a former music business executive turned author from New York City. He co-authored *The Merciless Book of Metal Lists* with Mass Appeal's Sacha Jenkins, *Misfit Summer Camp: 20 Years on the Road with the Vans Warped Tour* with Kevin Lyman and Hip-Hop Alphabet and Hip-Hop Alphabet 2 with Michael "Kaves" McLeer. Howie currently contributes to a number of music blogs, and co-hosts a weekly radio show called Merciless with rapper ILL BILL. Bad Brains is his all-time favorite band!

JAMES LATHOS is a filmmaker and published writer living in Florida. He makes his documentary debut with *Finding Joseph I: The H.R. from Bad Brains Documentary*, which is the primary inspiration for this book.

For more information about the **Finding Joseph I** *documentary film, go to* **HRdocumentary.com**